P.S. FOURNIER.

Né en 1712, mort en 1768.

The *Ars Typographica* Library
General Editor: James Moran

FOURNIER

the compleat typographer

Uniform with this volume
Roy Brewer : Eric Gill
Leslie Owens: J. H. Mason

ALLEN HUTT

FOURNIER

the compleat typographer

LONDON
FREDERICK MULLER LTD
1972

First published 1972 by
Frederick Muller Ltd.,
110 Fleet Street, London, EC4A 2AP

Copyright © 1972 Allen Hutt

Printed and bound in Great Britain
by W & J Mackay Limited, Chatham

SBN 584 10350 6

Contents

List of illustrations

The chapter heading vignettes are from a page in Monnet's *Anthologie Françoise* (Paris) 1765, using Fournier's music type

The intention of the *Ars Typographica* Library is to present to that section of the reading public interested in the art of printing, a series of books dealing with historically important printers; with those individuals who have made a major contribution to the "art preservative of all the arts"; and with tendencies in the art itself. Those who have assisted the progress of printing as an art have not always been printers: indeed, professional printers, with certain important exceptions, have not been outstanding in this respect. It has often been, on the one hand, the purveyor of printed matter, or, on the other, the supplier of printers' material, such as type, not to mention the complete outsider, who has influenced the course of change.

We have only to think of William Pickering, the publisher, who may never have printed a sheet of paper in his life, but whose skill as a book designer enhanced early nineteenth-century printing. There are those such as John Baskerville, writing master turned manufacturer of japanned ware, whose desire to contribute to the "Republic of Learning" caused him to become a printer, typefounder, ink and paper maker. Outstanding typefounders, such as William Caslon, have clearly assisted the art of printing, and we should not forget those who have designed types for the typefounder or the composing machine manufacturer. They have provided the typographer, or the graphic designer, with basic material with which to display the printed word to best advantage. The two kinds of artist are sometimes combined in one man and, just occasionally, there has been a printer who merits attention as type designer, typographer (in the modern sense of the word) and producer. Such men will not be overlooked in the series; but there was the question as to the choice of an outstanding figure with whom to begin. Bearing in mind the various disciplines which go toward the making of a distinguished piece of printing, there was little hesitation, since there was a man who comprehended the whole art, even if he was not allowed to practise it in its entirety—Pierre Simon Fournier, called *le jeune* (1712–1768), the master worker—"the compleat typographer" of Allen Hutt's title.

There was equally little hesitation in deciding who to approach to write the initial work. Both pedant and populariser had to be avoided if a complex subject was to be presented in a fashion acceptable to specialist and layman; and it was also thought desirable that the writer should be one who had a wide practical experience of the use of type, one who could appreciate fully the extent of Fournier's achievement. Fortunately, a man meeting these requirements was available in the person of Allen Hutt, who, as a journalist of more than forty years standing, has specialised in the typographical design of newspapers, and is the author of an indispensable handbook, *Newspaper Design*.

Mr Hutt had already written a sketch of Fournier's life and was well equipped to tackle the longer work, the more so since, by additional good fortune, he is also a scholar in the field of French history and literature, and of the eighteenth-century Encyclopaedists in particular. The importance of this background becomes apparent when Fournier's life and work are considered. While the eighteenth century may have been the age of enlightenment it was also a period during which guild privileges were vigorously defended, and Fournier, the innovator, had to work within a restrictive system. This being so, the achievements of his comparatively short life were remarkable. To assist in an appreciation of Fournier's work it would perhaps be useful to outline briefly the technical and aesthetic aspects of his profession.

For some five hundred years since typographic printing was invented in about 1440 by Johann Gutenberg of Mainz, reading matter has been printed from a raised surface, composed of pieces of type—that is, small metal blocks with letters in relief on the top. The invention of line-casting machines in the latter part of the nineteenth century, by which a whole line of such letters could be cast in one piece, does not alter the principle involved.

The making of these pieces of type is complicated, consisting, in essence, of casting pieces of metal of equal height in a mould. But the typecaster's mould is like no other, since each piece of cast metal has a relief letter on the top, which requires a mould of its own. This mould, known as a matrix, is incorporated in the main mould. Then, since letters of the alphabet vary in width, from I to W, the mould has to be adjustable. The making of the matrices is the major task.

A letter is cut in relief on the end of a small bar of steel, which is then known as a punch. This is a much simplified statement, as punch-cutting is not only a highly-skilled craft, but the craftsman has to have in his mind's eye the shape of the letter before he begins—a letter which must match the other letters and signs a printer will use. A study of type-faces (that is, the images created by type on paper) is necessary to see how successful, or otherwise, a punch-cutter has been.

After hardening, the punch is either struck or forced into a piece of copper to produce an intaglio version of the letter. This piece of copper is known as a strike, to which a laborious finishing process is applied to make it into an adequate matrix for casting type. This is because each piece of type cast must not only be of the same height as the others—to present an even printing surface—but the raised letter on the end must align with the rest of the alphabet in a way which will please the human eye.

The mould is made of two separate halves, which will slide parallel to one another to allow the insertion of any width of matrix, which is placed at the bottom of the mould and held in place by a spring. Molten metal is poured into the mould, which is shaken to force the metal into the matrix, and when the metal is hardened, is opened up and the type "sort", as it is called, ejected. Type metal is made from lead and tin and various alloys, to produce a freely running liquid which will penetrate into the extremities of the smallest matrix, and which, when hard, will allow ink to adhere and not reticulate.

While the hand-mould may still be used, from the middle of the nine-teenth century the process became mechanised. Towards the end of the century with the emergence of combined casting and composing machines, a new way of cutting matrices became necessary. The great number of matrices required if the combined casting and composing machines were to be a success could not possibly have been produced by the hand-punch method. Punch-cutting and matrix-engraving machines were devised to use patterns made by draughtsmen, who follow either the drawings of modern artists or photographic reproductions of the great type-faces of the past, including those of Fournier. The design of the types made by modern methods, therefore, is not inherent in the mode of manufacture. It comes from the nature of the written and hence the printed word, and some indefinable talent in the best punch-cutters and type designers who aimed and continue to aim at optical harmony.

In the period before the camera and matrix-engraving machine the punch-cutter was the type designer, and Fournier decided to learn the art of punch-cutting thoroughly to be able to produce the types he thought desirable, without the necessity of outside assistance. The results of his labours are documented in this book. As Mr Hutt says, his genius lay in his ability to modernise the traditional letter fo.ms, and his types are the first of the "transitional" between "old face" and "modern". His italics are considered to be his masterpiece.

But Fournier found there was no agreement between foundries on the "body" height of type. These heights or sizes had traditional names, which occur in the text following, and to which Fournier added others. For the benefit of readers an approximate equivalent in the modern point system is added in brackets after each name. Fournier, in fact, was the pioneer of a more rational system of type measurement (see chapters 2, 3 and 6), and while on the Continent it was largely replaced by that of F. A. Didot, by a curious accident of history his unit of 0.0135 inches approximates to the point of 0.0138 inches adopted by American type-foundries in 1886 and subsequently in Britain.

Modern techniques have enabled Fournier's typographical creations (types and flowers) to be reproduced for our use—this book is set in Monotype Barbou—and his point system and the concept of a "Type family", even if not so named, are with us still. When Fournier died, wrote Beatrice Warde (Paul Beaujon), he had made more changes in typography and set a more distinctive personal mark on the printed book than anyone else of his day. When in 1926 she wrote those words she also said that his roman and italic had lain fallow for a long time. That is no longer true. The products of Fournier's greatness are now available for all to see.

James Moran

For help in the preparation of this book, including the illustrations, I am indebted to James Moran, James Mosley, Helen Wodzicka and Alan Jones. Without the resources of the St Bride Institute Printing Library the work would not have been possible. For the convenience of reference the four works most frequently employed are cited in the following abbreviated form:

Updike: D. B. Updike, *Printing Types, their History, Forms and Use*, 2 vols., 1st edition (Harvard University Press, 1922)

Carter: Harry Carter, *Fournier on Typefounding*: the text of the *Manual Typographique* translated into English and edited with notes (London: Soncino Press, 1930)

Warde: Beatrice Warde (Paul Beaujon), *Pierre Simon Fournier and XVIIIth Century French Typography*, *The Monotype Recorder* Nos. 212–213, March–June, 1926 (London: The Lanston Monotype Corporation Ltd.)

Mosley: James Mosley, *An Introduction to Pierre Simon Fournier's Modèles des Caractères de l'Imprimerie* (supplement to collotype facsimile, London: Eugrammia Press, 1965)

As James Moran's Foreword notes, this book has been set—12 on 13 point—in Monotype Barbou (series 178), the Monotype Corporation's alternative to their Fournier (series 185), while display lines are in 185. The Barbou-Fournier mystery is discussed in chapter eight; comparative 9 point settings of the two type-faces appear on the following page.

Camden Town, July, 1972   G.A.H.

Barbou 178

On September 15, 1712 Mme Anne Catherine Fournier was brought to bed of her youngest son, Pierre Simon. It has often been remarked that this was also the year of the birth—some three months earlier—of Jean-Jacques Rousseau; but there was nothing in common between the son of the Parisian typefounder and the son of the Genevese clockmaker apart from their age and their French culture. Perhaps the author of the revolutionary *Contrat Social* and that educational masterpiece *Emile* might have appreciated Antoine Rivarol's later phrase—almost a wisecrack—that printing is "the artillery of thought"; certainly Pierre Simon Fournier would, as befitted one who, to continue the metaphor, became a true Master-General of the Ordnance.

Fournier 185

On September 15, 1712 Mme Anne Catherine Fournier was brought to bed of her youngest son, Pierre Simon. It has often been remarked that this was also the year of the birth—some three months earlier—of Jean-Jacques Rousseau; but there was nothing in common between the son of the Parisian typefounder and the son of the Genevese clockmaker apart from their age and their French culture. Perhaps the author of the revolutionary *Contrat Social* and that educational masterpiece *Emile* might have appreciated Antoine Rivarol's later phrase—almost a wisecrack—that printing is "the artillery of thought"; certainly Pierre Simon Fournier would, as befitted one who, to continue the metaphor, became a true Master-General of the Ordnance.

CHAPTER ONE

A family of typefounders

Auxerre is an old and tranquil French town on the river Yonne; it is the capital of the Department of that name. It has never been large—its present population is around 26,000—but it has been an urban centre for more than two millennia. Here the tribal hosts of Vercingetorix, the great Gaulish chieftain, rallied in 52 B.C. before their last disastrous campaign against Caesar and the establishment of unchallenged Roman rule over Gaul. Auxerre and the Yonne valley, indeed, is not merely a very old part of France's heartland; it is a very Gaulish part. To the south lies the wooded and strange region called the Morvan, a Celtic name if there ever was one. The Franks seem far away indeed.

In the seventeenth century, Auxerre was still a fortified town, though the circle of the fortifications has long since been replaced by wide, tree-lined boulevards. Within its walls there wrought a worthy family of printers, the Fourniers. Of this clan, one Jean Claude left Auxerre for the capital late in the century and turned from printing to typefounding. He learnt the trade in the establishment of Jean Cot, who had started his foundry in 1670 by buying up a number of small ones, and who had a respectable output of type-faces, later well shown in the 1742 specimen of Claude Lamesle, by whom they had been acquired. Jean Claude Fournier, however, must have had his eye on something more prestigious than Cot's foundry; and in 1698 he moved to the most famous foundry in France, conducted since the great Garamond days of the sixteenth century by successive generations of the Le Bé family. A few years later he was made manager and ran the foundry for the last Le Bé daughters until his death in 1729.

I

Now well-established in the typefounding business, Jean Claude married an Auxerre girl, Anne Catherine Guyon, by whom he had a large family. Of these, only the three boys who survived infancy need concern us here. The eldest, Jean Pierre (usually styled *l'aîné*) was born in 1706 and was to follow his father by buying the Le Bé foundry in 1730. The second, Michel François, went back to Auxerre as a printer; by the mid-1750s he appears to have been the only printer in the town and, what is more, had as one of his apprentices the astonishing Restif de la Bretonne, later a compositor at the Imprimerie Royale in Paris, who himself set his 16-volume novel *Monsieur Nicolas* ("or, the Human Heart Unveiled") in highly idiosyncratic fashion—using 12 point type for passion, 9 point for "boring but necessary details", and 8 point for "basic narrative". The Fournier printshop in Auxerre was continued by Michel François' son Laurent until 1824, and in 1930 Harry Carter described it as still extant, though under other ownership.[1] The third, Pierre Simon, commonly called *le jeune*, was born in 1712; he was to prove the most remarkable typographic artist of his age, and to him and his work the present book is devoted.

The Fournier family's typefounding connections were complex. Fournier *l'aîné* had a son, Jean François, and three daughters, Elizabeth Françoise, Marie and Adelaide. After their father's death in 1783 the daughters efficiently carried on the great foundry, true to the tradition of typefounder's womenfolk (think of the Caslon and Bodoni widows!) until it disappeared from history during the turmoil of the Revolution and the Napoleonic period; by the time Pierre Capelle wrote his *Manuel de la Typographie Française* in 1826 the working stock of punches, matrices and moulds had long been dispersed.

Fournier *fils*, as Jean François usually styled himself, set up as a type-cutter and founder on his own account. In 1767 he issued specimens of his types and ornaments and two years later advertised his wares in the *Mercure de France*; from the types he there listed Updike concluded that he "inherited some of his father's famous old characters".[2] This seems unlikely, since in 1769 *l'aîné* still had 14 years of activity ahead of him; but he may well have let his son have some strikes. In any event, Fournier *fils*

[1] Massin, *Letter and Image* (1970), p. 226: Carter, p. xv.
[2] Updike, I pp. 250–1.

survived his father by only three years, dying in 1786; and his type-founding business passed to his son-in-law Antoine François Momoro, a Paris printer.

Fournier *fils* had married Marie Elizabeth Gando, daughter of one of the French-Swiss typefounding family of that name, successive members of which had moved from Basle or Geneva to Paris from the early years of the century on (they were an unscrupulous family, and we shall see later how Fournier *le jeune* fell foul of them). The Fournier-Gando daughter Sophie married Momoro, who issued a specimen of "Some of the Types" from his foundry in 1787; he had already published an illustrated textbook, *Traité Elémentaire De l'Imprimerie, ou le Manuel de l'Imprimeur*. Updike dismissed this as "carelessly compiled"; but it was popular enough to have a second edition in 1793, brought out again in 1796 with a cancel title.

Evidently it was Momoro's "turbulent, visionary, unbalanced" politics that filled Updike with acute distaste. From 1789 on, the Fournier son-in-law stood on the extreme left of the French Revolution; associated first with Danton and then with the radical Hébert, he was so far in advance of his time that he preached Socialism during a tour of Normandy in 1792 and was denounced in consequence; with his fellow-Hébertists he was railroaded to the guillotine in March 1794—one of the last major acts of the Robespierre dictatorship before the Thermidorian reaction.[1] He had a son, who later assumed the name of Fournier, about whom nothing seems to be known.

Pierre Simon *le jeune*, the subject of this work, himself had a substantial typefounding sequel. His eldest son, Simon Pierre, 18 when his father died in 1768, was trained in his uncle's foundry; eventually he succeeded his mother, who carried on the Fournier *le jeune* business till her own death in 1775. Simon Pierre, also calling himself *le jeune*—uncle Jean Pierre *l'aîné* being still alive—issued a specimen in 1781 of a new script type "in the English style". The Birrell and Garnett *Typefounders' Specimens* catalogue of 1928 contained a portion of a unique specimen of Simon Pierre's dated January 1790; in 1804 Simon Pierre's son, the grandson of the great *le jeune*, Beaulieu-Fournier (Simon Pierre had married a Mlle de Beaulieu of Chartres) was listed as a typefounder living in the old Rue

[1] Updike, I p. 249n: Aulard, *Histoire Politique de la Révolution Française* (Paris, 1913) pp. 260–2, 463.

des Postes (now Rue Lhomond), in the heart of the *Quartier Latin*, immediately south of the Pantheon, which had been the Paris home and workshop of the Fourniers for many years.[1] By the Restoration, however, as with the foundry of *l'aîmé*, the establishment of *le jeune* had ceased to exist.

When Benjamin Franklin was American envoy in France during the War of Independence he had close connections with the Fourniers, both *l'aîné* and Simon Pierre; so friendly, indeed, was the latter that he arranged to have a portrait of Franklin painted at his own expense. Whether the portrait was ever painted, or what happened to it, is unknown; but some time later an American visitor to the Fournier foundry reported that it was adorned by a bust of Franklin, much admired by the French foundry-men. Franklin was anxious for his printer grandson, Benjamin Franklin Bache, to learn type-founding, and arranged for him to be trained by François Ambroise Didot. He also bought matrices and other material to set up a foundry for Bache on his return to Philadelphia. A specimen sheet issued by Bache around 1790 showed some types cast from Fournier matrices.[2]

These Fournier family proliferations need not detain us further. For the most part they were incidental to the determination of the intellectual and technical climate in which Fournier *le jeune* was to develop. What was important typographically around the end of the first third of the eighteenth century in France was: (i) what may be called the great survivals, of which the Le Bé foundry was an outstanding example; and (ii) the emergence of a new approach to letter-design which could reason-ably be called "scientific", or perhaps—as thoughtful men might then have said—"philosophical".

The Le Bé foundry, it has already been observed, stemmed from the classic days of French sixteenth-century typography. As directed by Fournier *père* and his eldest son it had, as Updike said, "a great reputation, and justly enough—for it was a noble collection of beautiful old types, cut by masters of French type design"; here were original punches and matrices

[1] Carter (p. xxxiii) speaks of Charles Fournier Desormes, "son of Simon-Pierre II" and later a painter and poet of some note, as reportedly owning the foundry at the end of the Napoleonic wars, but "probably" disposing of it before 1819.

[2] Updike, I p. 257, II pp. 152–3.

of Garamond himself, Robert Granjon, the first Le Bé, Jacques de Sanlecque. Curiously enough, throughout its long history, up to and including
the regime of Fournier *l'aîné*, the foundry never seems to have issued any
specimens; though some of its types were to be shown by Fournier *le
jeune*, as will be noted later.

Guillaume Le Bé I, born at Troyes in 1525, was a pupil of the great
printer Robert Estienne; he also worked in Rome and Venice and made
himself an unchallenged reputation as a cutter of "exotic"—particularly
Hebrew—characters. He had close associations with Claude Garamond
and when that master died in 1561 he was his executor, acquiring many
of his punches, matrices and other foundry material; of these he sold a
number to Plantin in Antwerp. Dying in 1598 he was succeeded by his
son, Guillaume II, who corresponded with Jan Moretus, Plantin's son-in-
law and successor, and continued to strengthen the foundry's repertory.
He too had a son, Guillaume III, the last of the male line, who likewise
developed the foundry soundly until his death in 1685; the foundry was
then managed on behalf of his widow until her death and the appearance of
Fournier *père*.

The first Le Bé had a talented pupil, Jacques de Sanlecque, who emu-
lated him as a cutter of Oriental founts; in 1596 Sanlecque began his own
foundry which was continued by his son Jacques, his grandson Jean and
his great-grandson Louis—who, in 1757, issued an elegant specimen "full
of charming type, some of it no doubt special productions of the first
Sanlecques, and other characters by old type-cutters" (Updike). After
Louis de Sanlecque died, in 1778, his widow Marie boasted to Benjamin
Franklin that she was "proprietress of a foundry which I dare assure you
is the finest in Europe".

Now for the significant new approach to letter-design, which culmin-
ated in the cutting of the famous *Romain du Roi* by Philippe Grandjean
in 1702 and the further refinement of its italic by Jean Alexandre in 1712.
The story of the design and cutting of this exclusive new type for the
Royal printing-house has often been told; and, of course, it is a real Louis
XIV story. But its importance is far other than the typographic crowning
of the reign of that super-monarch, the *Roi Soleil*; and so far as the commonly received story goes it is now clear that it had several defects which
it is possible to rectify. These will transpire in the course of the exposition

5

that follows. The rectifications are based on a detailed and scholarly study (1961) by M. André Jammes, translated and substantially reproduced in No. 1 (1965) of the *Journal of the Printing Historical Society* under the title "Académisme et Typographie".

The conception and gestation of the *Romain du Roi* was without precedent in the history of typography; but then the whole period was, intellectually, unprecedented. It was the age of Descartes and Newton, the age of organised development of scientific speculation and inquiry. In the 1660s the foundation of the Académie des Sciences in Paris shortly followed the establishment of the Royal Society in London. From the start, the Académie was urged to consider projects for an encyclopaedic survey of all *arts et métiers*, of arts and crafts and their techniques, thus prefiguring the *Encyclopédie* itself (though that was to be the independent, non-academic achievement of Diderot and his colleagues in the next century). The principal aim was the practical one of improving the level of craft techniques.

Eventually the work went to what we would call a sub-committee, in which Abbé Bignon of the Académie presided over three outside experts, Jacques Jaugeon, Gilles Filleau des Billettes and Père Sebastian Truchet. The "little academy", as they came to be called, set to in January 1693 and at once concerned themselves with "the Art which preserves all others—namely printing". Their researches met with academic approval, for in 1699 the three outsiders were made members of the Académie (with the status of *mécaniciens*) and in the same year the Académie gave this account of their work on typography:

"M Jaugeon . . . first of all gathered together alphabets of every language, both dead and living. . . . Next he showed the Academy a new French alphabet that had been chosen to please the eye as far as was possible. . . . It would hardly be believed what pains were taken to measure the proportions of height to width, the outlines, the space between the different parts which make up the shape of each letter. After consulting all the authors who have written upon this subject . . . we were reduced to consult principally the eye, the sovereign arbiter." To which it was added that Jaugeon and his colleagues had "devised a geometrical method by which workmen can execute the exact form of the letters they have designed with the utmost precision".

6

This "geometrical method" was based on the division and sub-division of a square into 2,304 small squares (for roman capitals); so the mistaken view arose that the letter-design of Jaugeon was a purely academic ruler-and-compass exercise—"worthless and impossible geometrical calculations" as Fournier *le jeune* himself was to call them many years later. In the *Manuel Typographique*, Fournier went to considerable lengths to demolish what he conceived to be a "hobble to genius" which could only "curb the mind and suppress taste". In particular he jeered at the "useless . . . multiplicity of lines" when it came to the minute work of punch-cutting. Thus the myth was propagated that, when Grandjean came to cut the punches for the *Romain du Roi*, his ingenuity as an "artist" fortunately circumvented the restrictions imposed by the academic "theorists".

Contemporary documentation recovered by M. Jammes shows that these traditional views were very much wide of the mark. Notes by Jaugeon himself leave no doubt that the 2,304-square grid was only intended to plot the preparatory large-scale patterns and had no relation to the actual punch-cutting, where "at least in the smaller sizes, it is very difficult to achieve perfect accuracy" and it is always "the eye of the craftsman that must decide". When the *Romain du Roi* reached the punch-cutting stage each letter was considered to be divided vertically into eight parts, as against the seven parts later prescribed by Fournier—a minor difference, it will be seen.

In any event the objective and historical approach of the "little academy" to their work was the direct opposite of any abstract, formal or "theoretical" attitude; it is enough to quote Jaugeon's words—"we began by making a collection of all letters made by punches and which have been approved of in the finest printed books. Next we consulted those writers who have tried to provide rules and proportions for them". Even more suggestive is Jaugeon's own account of the flexible approach of himself and his colleagues in the final stages of the type-design:

"We made letters of every size and proportion, for which we took our eyes as judges. . . . We believed, together with innumerable scholars . . . that a proportion of one to eight was the most elegant for the thickness of the capitals, and one to six gave the most pleasing proportion to the lower-case. But since large objects reduced to small ones often change in grace

PREMIERE PARTIE
LES ÉPOQUES.

PREMIERE ÉPOQUE.
ADAM OU LA CREATION.

Premier age du Monde.

L'intention principale de Bossuet est de faire obser-
ver dans la suite des temps celle de la religion et
celle des grands Empires. Après avoir fait aller
ensemble selon le cours des années les faits qui
regardent ces deux choses, il reprend en particulier
avec les réflexions nécessaires premièrement ceux
qui nous font entendre la durée perpétüelle de
la religion, *et enfin ceux qui nous découvrent les*
causes des grands changements arrivés dans les
empires.

La première époque vous présente d'abord un
grand spectacle : Dieu qui crée le ciel et la terre
par sa parole, et qui fait l'homme à son image.
C'est par où commence Moïse, le plus ancien

Grandjean's Romain du Roi *(1702)*

8

PREMIERE PARTIE
LES ÉPOQUES.

PREMIERE ÉPOQUE.
ADAM OU LA CREATION.

Premier age du Monde.

L'intention principale de Bossuet est de faire observer dans la suite des temps celle de la religion et celle des grands Empires. Après avoir fait aller ensemble selon le cours des années les faits qui regardent ces deux choses, il reprend en particulier avec les réflexions nécessaires premièrement ceux qui nous font entendre la durée perpétuelle de la religion, *et enfin ceux qui nous découvrent les* causes des grands changements arrivés dans les empires.

La première époque vous présente d'abord un grand spectacle : Dieu qui crée le ciel et la terre par sa parole, et qui fait l'homme à son image. C'est par où commence Moïse, le plus ancien des historiens, le plus sublime des philosophes, et le plus sage des législateurs.

Alexandre's refinement of Grandjean's italics (1712)

9

as well as in size, we observed in proofs made with punches that to many they appeared far too thin, and that by giving a proportion of one to seven to the first and one to five for the second, we were able to reach the end we were seeking and conclude to the satisfaction of the greatest number. . . . We should only judge the beauty and ugliness of things when they are shown in their normal size, and even this is not the same for everybody."

A second mistake—or, perhaps more correctly, over-simplification—in the appreciation of the nature of the *Romain du Roi* was the view that its design was inspired by the engraver rather than the calligrapher. Stanley Morison was of the opinion that the French academics considered printing to be "not a branch of handwriting but a branch of engraving". This view ignored the influence of contemporary calligraphy on the lettering of engravers like Simonneau (who engraved the large-scale "geometric" models for the *Romain du Roi*). There were great writing-masters in seventeenth-century France, like Nicolas Jarry and his successors; but they had developed a new style—"admirably elegant and accomplished", as M. Jammes says, with a general effect of "harmonious regularity", a marked contrast between thick and thin strokes and a non-cursive italic that we would call a sloped roman. The delicate skill of the engraver no doubt helped to popularise this new calligraphic style and thus had some influence on type-design; nevertheless the inspiration was still calligraphic.

To conclude: the production of the *Romain du Roi* was the result of the most remarkable and extensive piece of collective work in the annals of typography. That it was an exclusive "house" type did not detract from its importance as a watershed in type history. Here was the break with the traditions of the great Venetians, of Garamond and Granjon and the opening of the era of Fournier, Baskerville, Bodoni and the Didots. It was all very well for Pierre Simon Fournier, when an established master, to poke fun at Jaugeon; but the flowering of his own typographic genius took place in a France where the tone in type-design unavoidably stemmed from the projects of Jaugeon and his fellow-*mécaniciens* and their execution by Grandjean and Alexandre. Indeed, the extension of the *Romain du Roi* range was to be continued into Fournier's own early productive years by Louis Luce, Alexandre's son-in-law and successor as Royal punch-cutter.

CHAPTER TWO

The young Pierre Simon

On September 15, 1712 Mme Anne Catherine Fournier was brought to bed of her youngest son, Pierre Simon. It has often been remarked that this was also the year of the birth—some three months earlier—of Jean-Jacques Rousseau; but there was nothing in common between the son of the Parisian typefounder and the son of the Genevese clockmaker apart from their age and their French culture. Perhaps the author of the revolutionary *Contrat Social* and that educational masterpiece *Emile* might have appreciated Antoine Rivarol's later phrase—almost a wisecrack—that printing is "the artillery of thought"; certainly Pierre Simon Fournier would, as befitted one who, to continue the metaphor, became a true Master-General of the Ordnance.

Pierre Simon's upbringing was quite unlike that of his elder brothers, whom Fournier *père* put to their trades at the earliest proper moment and kept under his paternal eye during their training. Updike says he was the spoilt boy of the family, "living with his mother in the country until she died". As Mme Fournier did not die until 1772, four years after Pierre Simon (as disclosed in Updike's own Fournier family tree), this makes no sense. It was clearly Updike's mis-reading of a passage in the obituary *éloge* of 1770;[1] this says simply that "*une de ses parentes*", which can only mean "one of his female relatives" (Updike must have been confused by the dual aspect of the French word *parent*), prevented Pierre Simon from passing his childhood in the paternal home and kept him in the country until she died. Nobody has ever unravelled the mystery, nor are they likely to. We do not know who the doting relative was, nor where she

[1] *Nécrologe des Hommes Célèbres* (1770), pp. 231–51: *Eloge de M. Fournier le jeune.*

lived, nor how (and why) she got away with what seems a very odd business in terms of French family life.

Le jeune was 17 when, shortly before his father died in 1729, he returned to Paris. He joined his brother in the Le Bé foundry, presumably as a pupil or trainee and, either simultaneously or soon after, studied drawing at the Académie de St Luc; there his teacher was the miniaturist Jean-Baptiste-Gille Colson, a *Verdunois* then in his 40s. Why young Fournier went to the St Luc establishment instead of to the fashionable, and favoured, Académie Royale (founded by Le Brun and others in the mid-seventeenth century) must remain a matter of speculation. St Luc, which only assumed its academic title as part of its embittered campaign against the Le Brun organisation from 1648 on, was the medieval "mystery" ("mastery": *maîtrise*) of Paris painters—it took the sculptors in only in 1613—which dated back to the thirteenth century and was always battling for a sort of guild-monopoly "closed shop" in the arts. It proved too antiquated even for the *ancien régime* and was wound up in 1777. Nevertheless, Colson had a high reputation as a teacher and there is no doubt that *le jeune* learned a lot from him. Colson must have imparted much of his own delicacy and precision as a miniaturist to his pupil, who was to show such delicacy and precision as a letter-designer and punch-cutter.

Young Fournier was thus working hard at his drawing (and at wood-engraving), and was closely connected with a great typefoundry, at just that moment in eighteenth-century France when, as Beatrice Warde later wrote, "the general educated public had come to know something of type-founding: at least they knew there *was* such a craft"; as a result of the work of the academicians, of the Jaugeon-Grandjean *Romain du Roi* "this most cryptic trade came into the salon and was analysed and discussed".[1]

This was not a one-way process. While intelligent laymen were becoming conscious of the "cryptic trade", the "cryptic trade"—including printing with typefounding—was becoming conscious of itself. Pierre Cot, son of Jean Cot, the founder who was Fournier *père's* first master, began to publish details of his craft but died before he could complete them. And in 1723 a printer in the Flanders border town of St Omer, Martin-Dominique Fertel, published his *Science Pratique de l'Imprimerie*, the first

[1] Warde, p. 11.

French technical textbook. This 292-page quarto was quite exhaustive, starting with types and setting, showing how to display title-pages and make up a book, detailing the various schemes of imposition, discussing presses and presswork, paper and ink. In his preface the worthy Fertel indicated that his particular aim was to help apprentices and young journeymen to master their trade. His book was of more than local significance; not only did it secure the then customary Royal authorisation (*privilège du Roi*) but the official approval of the Paris master-printers. It must have come the way of young Fournier.

It was typical of the times that typography did more than invade the salons as a theme of conversation; to dabble in typesetting, and in working off presentation pieces on bijou presses, became the height of fashion. Royalty took the lead. From 1718–30 there was a miniature printing-office in the Tuileries which produced some 40 amateur items; one of these was a little geography primer on the rivers of Europe, described as set and printed by Louis XV when a child of eight. Much later Louis XVI, when the 12-year old Dauphin, produced 25 copies of a selection of "Moral and Political Maxims". The Pompadour herself was a devotee of printing and had a small press in her Versailles apartments (around 1760); one of her productions was, appropriately enough, that erotic master-piece the "Song of Songs".[1]

We know provokingly little of the seven years in Pierre Simon's life from his return at 17 to Paris (and work for his brother *chez* Le Bé) to his starting up on his own in 1736, at the age of 24. He soon made a name for his elegant woodcut ornaments (*vignettes de bois*), done for his brother; and he appears to have moved quickly on from wood to steel, cutting punches for large-size metal poster types. These *grosses de fonte*, usually cast with hollow bodies to save weight (and metal) ran, in modern equivalents, to around 108 point. From these large punches, comparatively easy to cut, it was a natural progression to the much more exacting task of cutting punches for the normal text sizes.

An autobiographical passage in the introduction to his first specimen book (the *Modèles* of 1742) indicates how studious and painstaking *le jeune* was in his approach to the design and manufacture of printing types. "I applied myself first of all," he wrote, "to discovering their beauties and

[1] Updike, I pp. 246–8.

NOUVELLE C

DE

LETTRES DE DEUX P.. ROM

ET DE REGLETS FILETS CROCHETS ET ACCOLLADES.

GROSSES DE

ABCDEF
MNOPQR

Ces trois fortes de Lettres
feront fonduës de façon que
le Corps en fera creux, afin
que l'Ouvrage en foit plus
leger, & l'Acquifition plus
facile.

XYZÆ

MOIENNES DE

ABCDEFGH
PQRSTUVX

Fournier's early metal poster types: reduced from a folding sheet in the 1742 Modèles: *the*
grosses *here are actually around 108pt (see p. 26)*

14

defects, and to remarking the changes to which they might be susceptible."
This led him, he went on, to consider mastering the art of punch-cutting
"so as to be able to work myself upon what I had remarked, without the
need of an alien hand". Thus he collected and studied proofs "of the most
beautiful types of different foundries, both in France and in foreign
countries. I took from each that which seemed good to me without following slavishly any one in particular". But, he stressed, he specially modelled
himself on the classic French type-cutters of the past ("foreigners have
never done anything as fine"), following their roman letter as nearly as
he could, "having care nevertheless to make certain changes which seemed
necessary to me".[1]

A pleasant picture emerges of Fournier poring over type-specimens
(and no doubt beginning to try his hand at large-size pattern-drawing).
The Le Bé foundry, even though it had no specimen books, must have
provided him with as many fount pulls of its classic types as he wanted.
Like everyone in the trade he was certainly familiar with, and impressed
by, the new-style *Romain du Roi* which, as already noted, Luce was extending and developing; in 1732 Luce produced a modification of Grandjean's letter, with simplified serifs, and noted the avid interest of other
Parisian typefounders, "who managed to get hold of every proof as fast
as it was completed for the Imprimerie Royale". Of the foreigners attract-
ing Fournier's attention the Dutch would have ranked high, though the
great seventeenth-century days of Van Dijck and Voskens were over;
he probably got an early sight of the large-faced, condensed roman, due to
develop into the eighteenth-century "Dutch style" (*gout hollandais*), of
which the first essay dated from 1734, the work of the German punch-
cutter J. M. Fleischman, working first in Amsterdam and later for the
Enschedés in Haarlem. By way of incidental comment here it may be
recorded that Fournier was later to refer (in the *Manuel*) to Fleischman
as "a very clever type-cutter" whose "work and talent" brought "very
considerable accessions" to the Enschedé foundry; on the other hand
Updike, hag-ridden by his hatred of the "modern" face and correctly
regarding Fleischman as one of its precursors, reviled him as "tasteless"
and "devoid of style".[2]

[1] Warde, p. 16.
[2] Updike, II p. 37.

15

S. AUGUSTIN ROMAIN.

L'air & les manieres rendent gracieux, dit M. l'Abbé Girard, l'esprit &
l'humeur rendent agréable. On aime la
rencontre d'un homme gracieux, il plaît;
on recherche la compagnie d'un homme
agréable, il amuse.

Les personnes polies sont toujours gra-
cieuses, & les personnes enjouées sont
ordinairement agréables.

Il semble que c'est plus par les manieres que par l'air que les hommes sont
gracieux, & que les femmes le sont
plutôt par leur air que par leurs manieres, quoiqu'elles puissent l'être par celles-
ci; mais il s'en trouve qui, avec l'air gracieux, ont les manieres rebutantes.

S. AUGUSTIN ITALIQUE.

A peine le nouvel hôte, dit le Pere
Brumoy, est-il entré dans l'édifice qui lui
est destiné, que, sans qu'il lui soit connu,
sans qu'il se connoisse lui-même, une se-
crete impulsion du corps l'avertit à coup
sûr de ce qui peut lui être avantageux ou
nuisible. Le plaisir & la douleur font l'ins-
tinct. L'un annonce le bien, & s'insinuant
jusques dans les moëlles, ce tendre moni-
teur persuade à l'esprit de chercher ce qui
convient au corps.

L'autre par un tact utile fait sentir la
présence du mal. Fuyez, s'écrie la douleur, l'ennemi n'est pas loin.

Louis Luce's 1732 modification of Grandjean's serifs; from Essai d'une Nouvelle Typographie *(1771)*

In 1736, then, *le jeune* was duly launched on his independent career as
a typefounder. His first specimen leaf, a *gros canon* italic (something above
our present 42pt) is dated that year,[1] in which he is also known to have
executed an order from the famous Barbou family, soon to become his
own printers, for a 350lb fount of type. Three years later he was formally
registered as a type-cutter and founder with the Paris printing trade
authorities.

The year after his start in typefounding Fournier performed what he
later called "the first homage which I rendered to typography". In 1737 he
drew up a "Table of Proportions" for printing types, his first essay in a
point system to bring order and standardisation into the traditional chaos
of type-body measurements. Before considering this historic step further
it will be useful to recall, for a generation which takes the uniformity of

[1] Mosley, pp. 10, 13.

typographic point systems for granted, just how anarchic the old position was.[1]

When Fournier wrote in 1742 that he was "perplexed to know what body height I should follow in each case, there being almost as many diversities of size as there were printing houses" he was only echoing complaints that Fertel had made in 1723. The "little academy" had sought to tackle the problem when it was working on the *Romain du Roi*, and secured a Royal order in 1694, though the proposed rules only applied to the Imprimerie Royale and do not (according to M. Jammes) appear to have been scrupulously observed.

The problem was just as acute in Britain. It worried Moxon (1683) and the printing textbooks of the eighteenth–nineteenth centuries, from John Smith (1755) through to William Savage (1841) continued the complaints, usually lifting the relevant passages from one textbook to the next, so unchanged was the situation. As late as 1890, Charles T. Jacobi, the manager of the Chiswick Press, could disclose a continuing chaos that seems scarcely credible. In *Printing*, the textbook which he contributed to George Bell's "Technological Handbooks" series, he reported that for the five leading founders of that day the long primer—our 10pt—varied in body between 89 and 92 to the foot; "the remaining sizes" he added, "are dependent very largely on these variations in long primer".[2]

Just what was the 1737 "Table of Proportions" and in what form was it issued? There has been some confusion about this, largely due to Updike. He spoke of "the tractate issued at Paris in 1737, entitled *Tables des Proportions qu'il faut observer entre les caractères*" (the Bigmore and Wyman bibliography listed as "Paris. 1737. 4to" the title *Table des Proportions des Caractères d'Imprimerie*).[3] Updike's supposed title occurs nowhere else, though some subsequent writers copied it from him; and, oddly enough, he admitted that he had never seen the "tractate" when he wrote "I do not know how the scheme of proportion of type-bodies proposed in the original formulation of 1737 compares with that proposed in 1742" (i.e. in the Table inserted in the *Modèles*). The only place that Updike can have read his wording was in the obituary *éloge* of 1770. The whole passage

---

[1] Warde, p. 26: Carter, pp. 291ff.

[2] C. T. Jacobi, *Printing* (London: Bell, 1890), p. 18.

[3] Updike, I p. 26.

TABLE
DES PROPORTIONS
DES DIFFERENS CARACTERES DE L'IMPRIMERIE.

Par S. P. FOURNIER, Graveur & Fondeur de Caractéres d'Imprimerie.

Nombre	CORPS.	ECHELLE DE ▭ DEUX POUCES.	Lig.es	Points
1	PARISIENNE.	. . . .		5
2	NOMPAREILLE.	. . . .	1	
3	MIGNONE.	. . . .	1	1
4	PETIT-TEXTE.	. . . .	1	2
5	GAILLARDE.	. . . .	1	3
6	PETIT-ROMAIN.	—— 2. Parisiennes.	1	4
7	PHILOSOPHIE.	—— 1. Parisienne , 1. Nompareille.	1	5
8	CICERO.	—— 2. Nompareilles. ‖ 1. Parisienne, 1. Mignone. .	2	
9	SAINT-AUGUSTIN.	—— 2. Mignones. ‖ 1. Nompareille, 1. Petit-Texte. .	2	2
10	GROS-TEXTE.	—— 2. Petits-Textes. ‖ 1. Parif. 1. Philofophie. ‖ 1. Nompareil. 1. Petit Romain. ‖ 1. Mignone, 1. Gaillarde. ‖ 2. Parif. 1. Nomp.	2	4
11	GROS-ROMAIN.	—— 2. Gaillardes. ‖ 3. Nompareilles. ‖ 1. Nomp. 1. Cicéro. ‖ 1. Mign. 1. Philofoph. ‖ 1. Pet. Text. 1. Pet. Rom. ‖ 2. Parif. 1. Pet. Text. ‖ 1. Parif. 1. Nomp. 1. Mignone.	3	
12	PETIT-PARANGON.	—— 2. Petits-Romains. ‖ 4. Parifiennes. ‖ 1. Nomp. 1. Saint-Augustin. ‖ 1. Pet. Text. 1. Cic. ‖ 1. Gaill. 1. Philofoph. ‖ 2. Parif. 1. Pet. Rom. ‖ 2. Nomp. 1. Pet. Text. ‖ 2. Mign. 1. Nomp. ‖ 1. Parif. 1. Nomp. 1. Gaill. ‖ 1. Parif. 1. Mignon. 1. Pet. Text.	3	2
13	GROS-PARANGON.	—— 2. Philofophies. ‖ 1. Nomp. 1. Gros-Texte. ‖ 1. Pet. Text. 1. Saint-Aug. ‖ 1. Pet. Rom. 1. Cic. ‖ 1. Parif. 1.Cic. ‖ 2. Nomp. 1. Pet. Rom. ‖ 2. Mign. 1. Pet. Text. ‖ 2. Pet. Text. 1. Nomp. ‖ 1. Parif. 1. Nomp. 1. Philofoph. ‖ 1. Nomp. 1. Mign. 1. Gaill. ‖ 2. Parif. 2. Nomp. ‖ 3. Parif. 1. Mignon.	3	4
14	PALESTINE.	—— 2. Ciceros. ‖ 3. Petits-Textes. ‖ 4. Nompareilles. ‖ 1. Nomp. 1. Gros-Romain. ‖ 1. Pet. Text. 1. Gr. Text. ‖ 1. Pet. Rom. 1. Saint-Aug. ‖ 2. Parif. 1. S. Aug. ‖ 2. Nomp. 1. Cic. ‖ 2. Mignon. 1. Pet. Rom. ‖ 1. Gaill. 1. Nomp. ‖ 1. Parif. 1. Mign. 1. Cic. ‖ 1. Parif. 1. Gaill. 1. Pet. Rom. ‖ 1. Nomp. 1. Mign. 1. Philofoph. ‖ 1. Nomp. 1. Pet. Text. 1. Pet. Rom. ‖ 1. Mign. 1. Pet. Text. 1. Gaill. ‖ 2. Parif. 2. Mign. ‖ 3. Parif. 1. Gaill.	4	
15	PETIT-CANON.	—— 2. Saints-Augustins. ‖ 4. Mignones. ‖ 1. Nomp. 1. Gros-Parangon. ‖ 1. Pet. Text. 1. Petit-Parangon. ‖ 1. Pet. Rom. 1. Gr. Rom. ‖ 1. Cic. 1. Gr. Text. ‖ 2. Parif. 1. Gr. Rom. ‖ 2. Nomp. 1. Gr. Text. ‖ 1. Mign. 1. S. Aug. ‖ 1. Pet. Text. 1. Cic. ‖ 1. Gaill. 1. Pet. Rom. ‖ 2. Pet. Rom. 1. Pet. Text. ‖ 2. Philofoph. 1. Nomp. ‖ 2. Parif. 2. Gaill. ‖ 2. Nomp. 2. Pet. Text. ‖ 1. Parif. 3. Nomp. ‖ 3. Nomp. 1. Pet. Rom. ‖ 4. Parif. 1. Pet. Text. ‖ 1. Parif. 1. Mign. 1. Gr. Text. ‖ 1. Nomp. 1. Pet. Text. 1. S. Aug. ‖ 1. Parif. 1. Gaill. 1. S. Aug. ‖ 1. Parif. 1. Philofoph. 1. Cic. ‖ 1. Nomp. 1. Pet. Rom. 1. Cic. ‖ 1. Mign. 1. Gaill. 1. Cic. ‖ 2. Nomp. 1. Mign. 1. Gaill. ‖ 2. Mign. 1. Nomp. 1. Pet. Text.	4	4
16	TRISMEGISTE.	—— 2. Gros-Romains. ‖ 3. Cicéros. ‖ 4. Gaillardes. ‖ 6. Nompareilles. ‖ 1. Pet. Text. 1. Petit-Canon. ‖ 1. Cic. 1. Palestine. ‖ 1. S. Aug. 1. Gr. Parang. ‖ 1. Gr. Text. 1. Pet. Parang. *(On peut encore augmenter de beaucoup l'affemblage de ce Corps & des fuivans.)*	6	
17	GROS-CANON.	—— 2. Gros-Parangons. ‖ 4. Philofophies. ‖ 1. Pet. Text. Trifmégifte. ‖ 1. Gr. Text. 1. Pet. Canon. ‖ 1. Pet. Parang. 1. Palestine.	7	2
18	DOUBLE-CANON.	—— 2. Petits-Canons. ‖ 4. Saint-Augustins. ‖ 8. Mignones. ‖ 1. Cic. 1. Gr. Canon. ‖ 1. Pet. Parang. 1. Trifmég.	9	2
19	TRIPLE-CANON.	—— 2. Trismegistes. ‖ 4. Gros-Romains. ‖ 6. Cicéros. ‖ 8. Gaillardes. ‖ 12. Nompareilles. ‖ 1. Gr. Text. 1. Doubl-Canon. ‖ 1. Pet. Can. 1. Gr. Can.	11	
20	GROSSE-NOMPA-REILLE.	—— 4. Palestines. ‖ 8. Cicéros. ‖ 12. Petits-Textes. ‖ 16. Nompareilles. ‖ 1. Palest. 1. Triple-Canon.	16	

Tous les Caractéres doivent avoir dix lignes & demie géométriques de hauteur en papier , fuivant les Réglemens ; ou onze lignes trois points , mefure de l'Echelle.	*Les Caractéres de l'Imprimerie n'ayant point eu jufqu'à préfent d'ordre parfait, (les Corps étant plus forts ou plus foibles, fuivant les Imprimeries) je leur donne ici un corps fixe & une correfpondance générale ; en confervant, autant que j'ai pû, les forces de corps ordinaires : ce qui a été approuvé des perfonnes les plus expérimentées dans l'Art. Et pour l'éxécution, j'ai fait une Echelle que je divife en deux pouces, le pouce en douze lignes, & la ligne en fix points ; où il faudra prendre exactement le nombre de lignes & de points que je marque pour chaque Corps.*

reads: in 1737 Fournier published his "savante Table des Proportions qu'il faut observer entre les caractères pour déterminer leur hauteur et fixer leurs rapports". In a footnote to his *Manuel de la Typographie Française* (1826) Pierre Capelle gave this full sentence in italics as if it were the 1737 title, while Updike chose, for some now undiscoverable reason, to stop short at the word *caractères*; it seems obvious that both of them misread the obituarist's description of the Table as if it were a title. It is significant that the title of the Table in the 1742 *Modèles* varied only from Bigmore and Wyman's supposed 1737 title by the insertion of the word *différents* before *caractères*. The conclusion seems inescapable; the Table of 1742 is the original Table of 1737; there was no "development" or change between the two dates; that only came much later, with the final form of the point system expounded in the *Manuel* of 1764. This is the view of James Mosley who advances the sound supposition that the Table in the *Modèles* "is reprinted from the same setting as the Table of 1737, for it incorporates sixteenth-century types from the foundry of Fournier *l'âiné* which would hardly have been used if the smaller types of Fournier *le jeune* had been ready".[1] Mosley's point is emphasised by the old face italics in the note at the foot of the Table, reduced opposite from the large folding sheet in the *Modèles*.

The "learned" Table of 1737, as reproduced five years later in the *Modèles*, was thus Fournier's initial essay in giving each body of type "a fixed and determined degree of depth and proportion which should be uniform" and thus avoid the grave "inconvenience" of mixing bodies of varying depth. He observed that he "established a regular gradation and a general inter-relation . . . so that the large bodies are precisely the double, triple or quadruple of those under them". There were, however, complications in Fournier's first scheme of proportions; the system was duodecimal, based on the division of the inch—the old French *pouce* was fractionally longer than the English inch—into 12 "lines" and each "line" into six points. Thus the unit was the "line"; *nompareille* (6pt) was therefore "one line", *cicéro* (12pt) "two lines", *St Augustin* (14pt) "two lines, two points". All sizes below 12pt had to be expressed on the line-and-point basis, as did all the bastard sizes, namely those that were not duo-decimal, above 12pt.

[1] Mosley, p. 4: see also Carter, p. xvii.

That this first scheme had its cumbersome aspects did not detract from its achievement, even though the *éloge* may be thought somewhat rhetorical when it proclaimed that the Table at once made Fournier "the Legislator of Printers". It not surprisingly brought him into conflict with interested parties among the typefounders, whom the ancient chaos often benefited (or was thought to benefit). *Le jeune* found himself the target of much criticism from those "blinded by ignorance or envy", as the obituarist put it. Fournier, as will be seen later, revelled in polemic, though on this occasion he does not appear to have bothered to answer his detractors; the *éloge* recounted, however, as if it were a matter of consequence, that the Table was warmly and publicly endorsed by the Abbé Desfontaines, a highly respectable littérateur of those days who (as it happened) was just about to tangle with Voltaire.

CHAPTER THREE

A six years' wonder

Fournier *le jeune* was not quite 30 when, in the summer of 1742, he published his first specimen book, the *Modèles des Caractères de l'Imprimerie*—"and of other things necessary to the said art, newly cut by Simon-Pierre Fournier *le jeune*, type-cutter and founder". It was only six years since he had started out in business and just over three years since he had officially registered with the Paris printing trade authorities. As Harry Carter said, "the output for six years is astounding"; the book showed 4,600 characters, all from punches cut by Fournier himself (no "alien hand" intervened, as the quotation in the previous chapter has indicated). The nature of the feat can be appreciated when it is understood that it meant the cutting of five punches every two days; the average time taken by a skilled, fast punch-cutter is reckoned at over a day a punch. Nor was this all. Fournier also had to strike and justify his matrices, as well as overseeing the work of the foundry as a whole—the casting and dressing of the types and the general conduct of the business. It has been suggested, most reasonably, that he could not have cut full founts of matrices for each size and style of type in the time and that most probably he only cut enough to provide the specimens in the *Modèles*, completing the founts later.[1]

The book, an oblong quarto with a spacious page, "was printed for Fournier by Jean Joseph Barbou, and is one of the most effective and elegant books of its kind ever issued in France" (Updike).[2] It was a decorative production, each page within a framework of varied arrange-

[1] Carter, p. xviii. Carter also gives a translation of the full text of the *Avis* (pp. 282–98).

[2] Updike, I p. 252.

21

ments of Fournier's flowers (to which the next chapter pays some attention). Many years later Fournier recalled that he himself had "set all the difficult and artistic parts of this book" and had himself transported the made-up pages to the printer.[1]

Ten copies of this outstanding specimen book are known to exist (that is to say, their location is known), the most complete being that in the St Bride Library, London. The St Bride copy has been issued in collotype facsimile with an introductory supplement by James Mosley, providing the most up-to-date and scholarly documentation of the *Modèles* to be had; among other things it analyses the significant variations between the different copies; to it the inquiring reader may be referred. The copy in the Royal Library, Stockholm, is that of J. G. I. Breitkopf of Leipzig, whose later association with Fournier in the revolutionising of music-printing is discussed in the next chapter.

Years afterwards Breitkopf told Fournier how he had first come across the *Modèles* in Berlin in 1742; it had been brought to the Prussian capital by C. F. Simon, a French printer called in by Frederick the Great to advise on the setting-up of a Prussian Royal Printing-house, and presented to the King. "Because of my admiration for the work I was given this selfsame copy as a present," Breitkopf wrote, "which I regard as an ornament of my library."[2]

The *Modèles*, indeed, were much more than an extensive and striking set of type specimens, exhibiting Fournier's letter design in its "fully evolved" state;[3] this is examined in detail below. They reproduced the famous Table of Proportions—the first version of Fournier's point system, already discussed. They were also prefaced by a ten-and-a-half page "Notice to devotees of the printing art" (*Avis aux amateurs de l'art de l'imprimerie*), set wide measure in the *gros romain*, or 18pt, size of Fournier's new and extremely handsome italic. The *Avis* was a kind of apologia, a statement of attitude and policy of a searching and quite unusual sort.

Fournier began by stressing the central importance for all printing from type of the art of punch-cutting ("perhaps the least known and least practised of all"). The steel punch had a long life and could be used to strike matrices as often as they might be wanted; only when punches were lacking, or when improvements were felt to be necessary—because some

[1] Mosley, p. 16n.　　[2] Quoted Mosley, p. 19.　　[3] Carter, p. xix.

letters were irregular or too out-of-date—was it necessary to cut new ones. This established, Fournier briefly recalled the fifteenth-century invention of printing in Germany, commonly ascribed to Gutenberg "though there are several other claimants"; he mentioned the development from the wood-block book to the devising of the matrix and the mould for casting separate types, and noted the evolution from Gothic to Roman typography as exemplified in the work of Aldus Manutius at Venice.

He then turned to expatiate, with some patriotic pride, on the great contribution to letter-design of the master punch-cutters of sixteenth- and early seventeenth-century France (for this purpose he made use of a document left by the second Le Bé, amplified by Jean Cot, his father's first employer in Paris). Brief sketches followed on the life and work of Simon de Colines, Claude Garamond, Robert Granjon, Guillaume Le Bé I, Jacques de Sanlecque and his son, Jean Jannon of Sedan (the man who first cut a 5pt, which he called *Sédanoise*, to be followed by de Sanlecque *fils* with his *Parisienne*, which became the common French name for this "the incomparably small" type).

So well did these masters succeed, Fournier went on, that their types became the models for fine bookwork not only in France but also abroad; "strikes from their punches found their way to various parts of Europe, where they are still used as successfully as in Paris. Thus it may be said that if Germany gave birth to the art of printing, France, and above all the City of Paris, carried it to perfection". The untimely death of the younger de Sanlecque in 1660 (he was only 46) removed the last of the great punch-cutters; for nearly 60 years punch-cutting was so neglected ("buried in obscurity", as Fournier put it) that when the capital J and U were introduced in French typography, in place of the I and V that had hitherto done duty for these consonant and vowel sounds, it was with difficulty that anyone could be found capable of cutting the necessary punches.

Here Fournier embarked on the piece of professional autobiography, and the advocacy of a standard point system for type-bodies, which have already been partly quoted in the preceding chapter. The pages in which he criticised the existing chaos in type-sizes and advocated a rationally proportionate and fixed system, were an exposition of the Table of Proportions appearing in the *Modèles*. He explained that, in thus seeking a firm and proportionate system of standardisation of type-bodies, he felt

23

MODÉLES
DES CARACTERES
DE L'IMPRIMERIE,

ET DES AUTRES CHOSES NÉCESSAIRES AUDIT ART.

NOUVELLEMENT GRAVÉS

Par Simon-Pierre Fournier le jeune, Graveur & Fondeur de Caractéres.

A PARIS,

Ruë des sept voyes, vis-à-vis le Collége de Reims.

1742

AVIS
AUX AMATEURS
DE L'ART DE L'IMPRIMERIE.

L'ART de graver les Caractères de l'Imprimerie, dont les Livres imprimés depuis son origine font les effets, est peut-être celui de tous qui est le moins connu & le moins pratiqué ; à peine y a-t-il ordinairement dans tout le Royaume sept à huit personnes qui l'exercent. En voici la raison : c'est que lorsque les Poinçons font une fois gravés, & qu'ils ont servi à frapper les Matrices, qui font les feules chofes dont on faffe ufage dans la Fonderie, ces Poinçons fe confervent toûjours dans la même beauté, & peuvent fervir à faire de nouvelles Matrices en tel tems que l'on veut. C'est pourquoi on n'a befoin de graver que quand on manque de Poinçons, ou que l'on cherche à renchérir les uns fur les autres, en corrigeant ce que les Caractères ont d'irrégulier ou de trop ancien, pour les porter à un plus haut point de perfection.

Tout le monde fçait que l'Art de l'Imprimerie a pris naiffance en Allemagne vers l'an 1440. On donne communément l'honneur de l'invention à JEAN GUTTEMBERG, Gentilhomme Allemand, quoique plufieurs autres le lui difputent. Les premieres impreffions furent faites avec des Planches de bois, fur lefquelles on gravoit le difcours que l'on vouloit imprimer ; mais on s'apperçut bientôt des inconvéniens que cette maniere entraînoit après elle, parce que les Caractères étant indivifibles, il falloit graver continuellement, & on ne pouvoit corriger

A

he was entering into the spirit of the Royal Ordinance of 1723 and subsequent regulations, which had aimed to bring order and precision to printing types, and more particularly had fixed their height-to-paper.

Observing that all his types were cut in accordance with the Table of Proportions, Fournier explained the justification-gauge he used to check the accuracy of body-size and noted the advantage for the printer of standard and proportionate quad sizes (thus saving time in whiting-out pages) and of the ease with which superior letters or figures could be justified (in an 18pt line, say, a 6pt superior only needed a 12pt space beneath it). Printers who appreciated the advantage of standard proportions, as here expounded, would only have to order types so cut and cast when renewing their founts, "and so their printing-offices would insensibly find themselves in a perfectly sound state, without it costing them any more". Equally, typefounders would be able substantially to reduce the great numbers of moulds that they were compelled to maintain to please all their customers, a constant source of constraint and error.

The *Avis* continued by drawing the customers' attention to certain new and unusual sizes shown in the collection. These included *Trismégiste* (36pt), or two lines of *gros romain* (18pt), a size barely known, Fournier commented, other than in Fertel's textbook. *Palestine* (24pt), "hardly more known, and yet nevertheless an excellent size, being two lines of *cicéro* (12pt), the type most extensively used in printing." *Gros texte* (16pt), representing two lines of *petit texte* (8pt) was "entirely new"; its constitution, Fournier indicated, was related to his proportionate scheme and the fact that hitherto there had been no two-line *petit texte*.

Finally, said the *Avis*, the specimens showed a new collection of two-line titling capitals, both roman and italic, "the last of which have been almost entirely lacking in the printing trade, with the exception of the Imprimerie Royale", whose types "perpetually honoured those who cut them". There were nine sizes of these roman and italic titlings, ranging from 12pt (two-line *nompareille*) to 72pt (two-line *Trismégiste*). There were also the formidably large cast poster types, the *grosses et moyennes de fonte*, already mentioned as among Fournier's early efforts in typefounding; the sizes shown, approximately 108pt and 84pt, were the largest metal types yet. "I did them," said Fournier, "so as to make good, at least up to this size, the crude and inevitable defects always found in wood letter."

With a certain smugness he added that the cutting of these two-line titlings showed that he took into account "the embellishing of the printed job rather than my own interests, since these types cost us most and bring in least". The market for them was highly selective and a single assortment would last a printer for life.

However, Fournier declared, since these types provided some extra adornment, he had not hesitated to cut them; and the same applied to his flowers (*vignettes*) which could either be used singly or made up together to form "different designs which can be infinitely multiplied". Also in the field of decoration, he noted that he had devised a mould to make single, double or treble rules of all lengths (up to 14 inches) and on all bodies; these cast rules are "more suitable than the brass rules commonly used, and at half the price".

Fournier concluded that his foundry offered all the usual signs, figures and the like needed by the printer; he undertook to cut any "specials" to order. In an amiable, self-critical final sentence, he wrote: "It remains for me to examine all my types anew, in order to correct any shortcomings that might have escaped me; I will do this as precisely as possible, so that I may give my types the highest degree of perfection that I can; indeed I would be most happy if, as a result of care and application, I could contribute in some measure to increasing the distinction which the printing trade of France, and above all that of Paris, has already rightly acquired."

Apart from the giant poster types and the two-line titlings, the *Modèles* showed a score of sizes in upper- and lower-case, text and display, ranging from *nompareille* (6pt) to *grosse nompareille* (96pt), all but the two largest sizes with italic as well as roman. Three of the large display sizes, including the *grosse nompareille* and the *triple canon* (72pt), were not Fournier's at all, but Le Bé faces from the late sixteenth and early seventeenth century, the matrices no doubt borrowed from the Le Bé collection in his elder brother's foundry.[1] One other display size, the *double canon* (56pt), had a Le Bé roman lower-case, with Fournier capitals, and a Fournier italic.

In view of what has already been said about the immense work put in by Fournier for the cutting and casting of his collection, it is hardly

[1] Mosley, p. 7ff.

surprising that he should have filled in these few gaps with classic old faces. No doubt his intention was, as opportunity offered, to replace them with his own designs. The two largest sizes, however, were never replaced; these Le Bé types were to be shown, more than 20 years later, in the *Manuel*. Clearly Fournier had been too busy extending and varying the sizes in more common demand; in those days the market for 72pt and 96pt display, with lower-case, must have been small indeed.

These understandable borrowings are really of quite minor consequence in respect of the great achievement presented in the *Modèles*. For these "fully evolved" designs of Fournier marked a watershed in typography; they were the first of the "transitional" faces, antedating Baskerville by more than a decade. As Beatrice Warde wrote: "no more happy compromise has been found between 'old' and 'modern' styles . . . so cleverly does it mingle tradition with precision of cutting that it seems at times to partake of almost contradictory virtues It is smart but not forward, old-fashioned but not archaic." In the same passage she applied the somewhat pejorative word "derivative" to the types of the *Modèles*, while immediately adding that they were "wonderfully sure in adaptation". Geoffrey Dowding carried this further by saying that Fournier "is not to be considered as an innovator of new type designs but rather as a clever adapter of the work of others". And Updike took the view that Fournier's types "do not now seem to us very novel. His roman is an old style character sharper in cut than that commonly in use at his period. . . . In his italic Fournier abandoned the whimsicalities so agreeable in old style founts, and made practically a *sloped roman* with a trimmed, mechanical line". Later on Updike spoke of Fournier "polishing the life out of the italics".[1]

These criticisms seem to be beside the point—and, indeed, to miss it. What type faces are not "derivative"? Good type designers do not start with a sheet of blank paper and an abstract, mystical inspiration. They begin, as Fournier did, by close study of, and careful thought concerning the best that has gone before. Historically, too, they have been profoundly influenced by the calligraphy of their time. Fournier was obviously influenced by the French sixteenth-century masters, and more nearly by Grandjean's *Romain du Roi*, with the subsequent work of Alexandre and

[1] Warde, p. 17: G. Dowding, *An Introduction to the History of Printing Types* (London: Wace, 1961), pp. 61–3: Updike, I pp. 257–9, 263.

28

Luce; but to write him down as a "clever adapter" is to underestimate entirely the meaning of his artistic achievement.

Fournier's genius lay in his ability to *modernise*—in the typographical sense of "modern"—the traditional letter forms. This went far beyond the "sharper cut" of an old face mentioned by Updike. The thin-thick stroke contrast was increased; flat, unbracketed serifs were introduced (as most strikingly shown in the *grosses et moyennes de fonte*); "interest has shifted," said Harry Carter, "from flowing curves to sharply-cut angles." Fournier's own description of his design changes, in the *Avis*, noted that he had levelled up the capitals with the lower-case ascenders (as against the ancient custom of making them slightly smaller) and went on: "I squared the angles of these same capitals a little more, as well as some of the lower-case letters, where I removed a certain rounding-off in the angle between the perpendicular and horizontal strokes. This serves to give them much more freedom, to distinguish one from another, and to make the strokes more clear."

The italics in the *Modèles* were, however, Fournier's masterpiece. Their originality and quality exceed that of his roman. They have been hailed as "the most legible of all italics" (Carter).[1] Their inspiration can certainly be seen in Alexandre's development of Grandjean's italics; but what Fournier did was to harmonise his italic with its roman. This was because, to quote Harry Carter again, he "approximated his italics to the prevailing round fashion in handwriting". Let us cite Fournier's own words from the *Avis*: "The difference that may be found between my italics and those of former times (most of which are still in use) is much greater [than those of the roman]. In several founts one may recognise the hand of the great masters who made them, by the sureness and equality of the strokes; but one may also observe a certain old-fashioned air which I have thought fit to reform. It is for this reason that I have followed my own taste in respect of these types by bringing them a little closer to our style of writing and,

---

[1] Carter, pp. xix–xx. Half a century later Momoro, paying tribute (around 1792) to Fournier's "wit and genius", specially stressed his italics, describing them as "effecting an advantageous revolution in printing", since "The old italics were bad, poorly cut. M. Pierre-Simon Fournier gave them a new form more agreeable to the eye. The old italics were soon abandoned everywhere, and his italics substituted for them" (*Manuel de l'Imprimeur*, pp. 103, 215).

above all, by clearly distinguishing the thick and thin strokes" (*distinguant bien surtout les pleins et les déliés*; in her 1926 Fournier study in the *Monotype Recorder* Beatrice Warde slipped over the last word, mis-translating it as "serifs"—*empattements* in French—and thus obscuring the point that Fournier was making).[1]

The special quality of Fournier's italics deserves to be emphasised Updike's dismissal of them as "sloping roman, with a mechanical, trimmed line" seems wide of the mark. More perceptive was Beatrice Warde's comment that Fournier's "sensitive taste" had transformed the Alexandre-Luce italic innovations of 1712–32 into "a face of considerable smug charm, a face, moreover, decidedly the italic *of a roman*: made to harmonise, that is, with an upright face. Whatever Robert Granjon's ideas of harmony were, he did not regard italic as the second half of a complete fount of type, but rather as a distinct letter, *combinable with* (rather than *inseparable from*) the same size of roman".[2] Curiously enough, despite this ingenious harmonisation, eighteenth-century French printers frequently used Fournier's popular italics with Garamond or other old face romans.

To examine in a little more detail the letter-design of Fournier's romans in the *Modèles* is to appreciate that his treatment was tolerably conservative. Compared with his old face predecessors, as James Mosley has remarked, "the colour and proportions are not radically different, and there is a pronounced oblique stress to 'c' and 'e', but the serifs are thin, straight and unbracketed, the 'b' has a foot serif, and there is a crisper, more regular air to the whole fount which reflects the geometrical curves that are the basis of the *Romain du Roi*, without being in any way a direct imitation."[3] Beatrice Warde thought that the *petit parangon ordinaire* (20pt) was notably successful—I think the same point could be made about a text size like *cicéro* (12pt)—with its "jaunty look"; "the flattened top of the 'a' and the tilt of the 'i' change the page as much as the larger bowled 'e' and unbracketed bottom serifs on the capitals. The 'last stroke' serif (bottom right) on the 'u' and the 'd' no longer slants upward, and . . . the lower-case 'j' differs from its predecessors by the straightening of a curve, so cleverly done as to justify in one stroke the designer's resolution to execute his own ideas from start to finish".[4] In his italic range Fournier offered certain alternative forms—as Luce did—such as modified long 's' (with

[1] Warde, p. 21.   [2] Warde, ibid.   [3] Mosley, p. 14.   [4] Warde, p. 17.

ascender but no descender; a curious kind of betwixt and between letter)
and a cursive '*d*' and '*g*'.

The *Modèles* were the first demonstration of two variations which
Fournier was to develop most extensively. The simplest was the casting
of a given size on a larger body; in the *Modèles* the *autre petit parangon*
(20pt) is a larger-body casting of *gros romain* (18pt), while the *autre gros
romain* is a comparable casting of *gros texte* (16pt). This device was an
obvious time and material-saver for a printer who needed to present a
given text 2pt leaded. More complex, and more interesting, were the
variations of style in a given size; here Fournier was beginning the trend
to the modern type "family", with its light, bold, condensed versions of
the same basic design. The start in the *Modèles* was modest enough; by the
time the *Manuel* appeared, more than 20 years later, there were no fewer
than ten variants of *cicéro* (12pt) alone, as will be seen below. In the three
main text sizes of *petit texte* (8pt), *petit romain* (10pt) and *cicéro* (12pt) the
French printer of 1742 had a choice of normal weight (*ordinaire*) with its
italic, or large-face (*gros oeil*). In the case of *cicéro* Fournier offered him a
further middle-weight (*moyen*) as well—a remarkably subtle piece of
modification. The three large-face variants were most skilfully realised by
increasing the x-height and yet not giving the effect of over-shortening the
ascenders and descenders.

With these four variants the *Modèles* offered 12 romans in the normal
text range of 6, 7, 8, 9, 10, 11, 12 and 14pt (*St Augustin*), with eight italics;
while the large-text, and display, range up to 24pt—covering the equivalents of 16, 18, 20, 22pt—was a good deal more than printers in our day
have ever been accustomed to.

The *Modèles* boasted one "exotic"—two sizes of Hebrew, which to a
gentile eye look well cut. Fournier modelled them, as he says, "on the
finest manuscripts in the Royal Library" for a "considerable work" of the
Reverend Fathers of the Oratory. He cut them the year before the appearance of the *Modèles* and seems to have been rightly proud of them.

Pretty well as exotic, though not forming part of the *Modèles*—it is
noticed here because a specimen leaf is inserted in the facsimiled St Bride
copy—was Fournier's remarkable formal script, the *Caractère de Finance* or
Bâtarde Coulée. The specimen is dated 1749, though much later Fournier
wrote: "In 1752 our printing houses had need of a type which should

31

Fournier's formal script type

imitate present-day handwriting. I engraved two of these after Rossignol, the celebrated writing-master. The type had such success that in quite a short time I had enriched 47 printers throughout the kingdom." Fournier was not, in fact, out to imitate the current hand of everyday life but the formalised script of the scrivener or the engraver; it was a remarkable *tour de force*, with its swash terminals, alternative characters and fantastic shapes. The 1749 leaf advertised it as "for the use of novelty-seeking printers, for the impression of certain ephemeral pieces to which one might wish to give the appearance of writing". Circulars, tickets, invitations, all manner of ceremonial, judicial and financial items were listed as eminently suitable for the new script. With it Fournier provided a special series of *Lettres Ornées*, decorated italic capitals of great charm—apparently the first of the series of decorated faces for which he was to become famous— "to take the place of small caps" with *Bâtarde Coulée*.[1]

In the same year as the imposing *Modèles* Fournier issued a small-format specimen, the vest pocket-sized *Caractères de l'Imprimerie*. Though it consisted of no more than 42 leaves, printed one side only, in 24mo it included the principal types displayed in its quarto companion, the very largest sizes apart. Its economic format and paging must have paid off in a wide circulation throughout the overseers' boxes and composing rooms of Paris and doubtless the main provincial printing centres as well.[2] It is reproduced at the end of this work. The two specimen books, large and small, were "well received and established Fournier *le jeune* as a type-founder of importance. He added steadily to his stock, and became embroiled in a series of controversies about the state of printing in France, plagiaries of his own types and the monopoly of music printing enjoyed in France by the Ballard family".[3] The two chapters that follow will have more to say on these matters.

[1] Warde, pp. 28–30: Mosley, p. 16. In the *Manuel* (II p. 264) Fournier himself gave the date of 1741 for the cutting of the *coulée*; the larger (36pt) *Bâtarde* was probably the later cut.

[2] An introductory note in 6pt opened with the words "these types are cut in a consistent and uniform style" and expressed the hope the booklet might be helpful to many readers in acquainting them with type-names. For larger display of the types and extra items readers were referred to the "quarto collection" (the *Modèles*) and mention was made of the introductory *Avis*.

[3] Mosley, p. 16.

CHAPTER FOUR

Flowers—and music

More than anyone Fournier knew how to say it (typographically) with flowers. Harry Carter called him the "supreme master of typographic ornament". Beatrice Warde, an ardent devotee of printers' flowers said that Fournier's had "never been surpassed".[1] Nor was this praise limited to posterity; it had begun with his contemporaries. The obituary *éloge* of 1770, itemising Fournier's achievements in type-cutting, concluded with what was practically a paean to "above all, his type-metal ornaments" (*vignettes de fonte*). They are exemplified on pages 79, 86.

Fournier himself wrote in the *Manuel* that these cast decorative units "form a part of the art that our old engravers neglected. . . . It is only in the past 30 years that printing has been enriched in this respect, first by the engravers of the Imprimerie Royale and secondly by what I have provided in this line for the other printing-houses of the country". This was, perhaps, not quite fair to the "old engravers"; in the sixteenth-century French printers had led in the translation into typecast units of the arabesque motifs that the Renaissance adapted from the East. But these flowers were for use as single items of decoration or in formal strips and bands; what Fournier did was to design units which could be arranged in an infinite variety of combinations and patterns "in freedom limited only by the compositor's imagination" (Warde).

Fournier was not the first in this field, as shown by his reference to the Imprimerie Royale engravers. He meant Louis Luce, whose 1740 specimen of his then sensationally small *perle* (4pt) type[2] showed a whole number of

---

[1] Carter, p. xx: Warde, p. 23.

[2] Updike correctly stated that Luce's micro-type was named *perle* (I p. 246) but

flower ornaments cast on the same body together with their make-up into some delightfully rococo sprigs and sprays. These flowers no doubt inspired him; but his inventiveness, imagination and superior technical skill produced by far the most brilliant repertory of decorative units and the most representative of the gay and graceful style of the French eighteenth century.[1] It is noteworthy that Fournier did not appear to regard his flowers as a sort of afterthought; his earliest specimen books contain a great display of new ornaments to match his new types. The 1742 *Modèles* showed, in two folding sheets, many lively arrangements of his flowers to form head- and tail-pieces, factotum initials and the like; equally engaging ones were to be seen in his small format specimen of the same year, the *Caractères de l'Imprimerie*.

The eighteenth century, notably in France, was the age of the copper-plate engraver; and the decorative style developed by engravers like Cochin and Moreau had an undoubted influence on Fournier. His achievement was to provide the material by which comparable decorative effects could be secured in an ordinary letterpress printing surface. Among other things this ensured economy in working, since (except in the case of the extremely expensive fully-engraved book) the use of copperplate embellishments involved a separate impression. The point was well summarised by the French printing historian, F. Thibaudeau, when he referred to Fournier's flowers as "pieces susceptible of forming varied decorative arrangements, of a definite note and style, conceived with such foresight as to their use, that they lent themselves as well to the irregular curves of

---

unfortunately his table of type-names and point equivalents (I p. 27) brackets *perle* with *Parisienne* as 5pt; any French textbook gives it as 4pt (e.g. F. Thibaudeau, *La Lettre d'Imprimerie* (1921), I p. 300). Updike must have been thinking of the old English pearl, which was 5pt. He made a similar slip by equating English diamond ($4\frac{1}{2}$pt) with French *diamant*, which was 3pt.

[1] "Luce's flowers . . . are all too obviously based on the detail of wood-engravings . . . Fournier had a few set pieces, the vignette used on the binding of some copies of the *Modèles*, for example, that might equally well have been cut on wood. But his finest achievement was the creation of a series of flowers on a wide variety of type bodies for use together (here he reaped the benefit of his standard sizes), so that a complex and curvilinear system of ornament could be built up, which is recognisably of its period" (Mosley, p. 16).

CHANSONS CHOISIES.

I.

DE THIBAULT, COMTE DE CHAMPAGNE,
Roi de Navarre. (1)

LAS ! fi j'a - vois pouvoir d'oubli - er

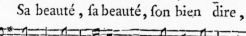

Sa beauté , fa beauté , fon bien dire,

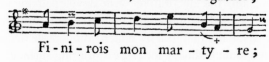

Et fon très-doux, très-doux regarder,

Fi - ni - rois mon mar - ty - re ;

(1) Sur cet illuftre Chanfonnier, & fur tous ceux dont les Couplets n'ont point de Notes particulieres , il faut confulter la Préface.

Fournier's petite musique *used in the* Anthologic françoise *(1765)*

escutcheons, rosettes and tail-pieces, as to form and decorate initials and framework; in a word, of being substituted for the corresponding employments of copper-plate engraving, while presenting the very appreciable advantage, for semi-de luxe editions, of economy of impression".[1]

Candide-like, Fournier constantly cultivated his typographic flower garden; in 1742 the *Modèles* showed 118 varieties while a score of years later the *Manuel* showed 377, available on no fewer than 13 bodies, from *Parisienne* (5pt) to *Trismégiste* (36pt). As Updike said, "At first glance, the larger, more obvious decorations, such as those of *gros-romain* (18pt) size, are the ones that strike us—frameworks with festoons, broken by bunches of flowers or knots. These are not more remarkable than the smallest ornaments—numbers 1 to 93 (5–8pt)—from which most charming effects were derived." Some ornaments could be arranged to form light-coloured

[1] Quoted Updike, I p. 260.

36

grounds on which bolder designs could be built up; many consecutive units were bracketed to indicate the possibilities of combination; there were a number of near-pictorial items, like sunbursts, medallions, garlands, all in all, to quote Updike again, "these ornaments became, in Fournier's hands, something almost as delightful as engraving, and yet wholly new".[1]

Fournier even contrived to give shape and style to conventional items of display like brackets or braces (*crochets* or *accolades*). His plain braces had lively curvature and colour; additionally he showed them in shaded or highly decorated forms. The *Manuel* offered ten varieties of metal rule, single, double and treble; with his continuous lead-and-rule mould innovation he could supply these in up to 14-inch lengths.[2]

In decorative alliance with Fournier's flowers were his decorated types. Fancy types had been known before; the English Union Pearl (still available from the Stephenson Blake foundry) dated from the 1690s and had lower-case as well as caps. What Fournier did was to pioneer the real *lettres de fantaisie* in a series of two-line titlings, in both roman and italic, ranging from a plain shaded letter of quiet elegance to the most gaily floriated and fantastic faces. In between was a "pearly" letter (the two-line *petit romain*, or 10pt) the italic of which was revived by the Deberny and Peignot foundry in Paris in 1913; this revival was designated "Fournier-le-Jeune" and was one of the exotics installed by Francis Meynell at his Pelican Press (in 1923 he wrote that these "decorated capitals are manifestly for special and discreet use. So used . . . they have been 'the making' of more than one seemingly intractable job".)[3] In Germany in 1922 the designer P. A. Demeter produced Fournier—a flowery, open titling fount. The reader may refer to page 70 below.

Fournier's mastery of typographic decoration was exceptional; but it was not novel—he simply did much better and with incomparable flair what others had been, and were, doing. The case was far different with his work on music types; here he, side by side with German and Dutch

---

[1] Updike, I pp. 264-5.

[2] Thibaudeau aptly commented that "one of the principal proofs of Fournier's taste was the care he took over the smallest details of typographic decoration"—in respect of rules, dashes, braces and the like (*La Lettre d'Imprimerie*, I p. 295).

[3] *Typography*—"compiled and for the most part written by Francis Meynell, the Typographer of the Pelican Press"—(1923) p. xviii.

innovators like Breitkopf, Rosart and Fleischman, pioneered the complex achievement of revolutionising both the typography and the printing of music. For Fournier, too, this was a great deal more than a technical triumph; it involved him in his biggest single battle against professional obscurantism and vested interest; this likewise embroiled him in embittered polemic with unscrupulous trade competitors such as the Gando family, mentioned in an earlier chapter.

The technical problem tackled by Fournier and the others was to bring the quality of type-music up to the elegant, rounded notation developed by the music-engravers; a further aim was to avoid the need for two work-ings—staves first, notes overprinted afterwards. In the musical eighteenth century, too, there was the consideration that hard founders' metal would stand up to much longer runs than the engraved music, often on soft pewter plates.

The whole story is a fascinating one. Within recent years it has been fully recounted in an authoritative study by H. Edmund Poole in the *Journal of the Printing Historical Society* (No. 1, 1965 and No. 2, 1966). Much of what follows is taken from his scholarly survey and to it the reader interested in the complex byways of musical typography may be referred. Here we need do no more than note the claim of Jacques François Rosart of Namur to be the first in the field (with a music type for the Enschedé foundry in Haarlem in 1750), to the later work of J. M. Fleisch-man for Enschedé (when Leopold Mozart visited Haarlem to discuss the elaborate music fount Fleischman cut to illustrate his work on violin-playing, he was accompanied by his prodigy son Wolfgang Amadeus, who slipped away to the Groote Kerk to exercise himself with a voluntary or two on the organ that is still there), to the efforts of the Swede Henric Fougt (both in Stockholm and London).

While Fournier was well aware of the work done at the Enschedé foundry, which he mentioned in some detail in the *Manuel*,[1] his main concern was with Johann Gottlob Immanuel Breitkopf of Leipzig, who may properly be considered the outstanding new music-type pioneer. Breitkopf announced his new method of music printing at the beginning of 1755; he and Fournier were soon in friendly correspondence on this project, which was unusual for the Leipziger, who generally resented the

[1] *Manuel Typographique*, I pp. 50–52.

efforts of those he regarded as rivals (especially Fleischman).

The first letter from Fournier to Breitkopf was warm in its praise of the precision and accuracy of the new music characters while asserting that he himself had been thinking on similar lines for some time. In 1754, Fournier added, he had already decided to devise new music types much like Breitkopf's, but was deflected by matters that he felt more urgent. Next year (1756) Fournier sent to Breitkopf one of the 12 copies he printed of an *Essai d'un nouveau caractère de fonte pour l'impression de la musique*. This was his first showing of music type; he later called it his "first music". It was a halfway house. He cut 30 punches for what he described as "the trial or draught of characters proper for printing at one impression"; but this "first music" was still a double impression job.

When Beatrice Warde wrote on Fournier in 1926 she could do no more than mention the *Essai*, since no copy was then known to have survived. There is, however, a unique copy in the Swedish Royal Library (most likely the actual copy sent to Breitkopf). In the *Essai* Fournier exposed the backwardness and decay of French music printing resulting from the monopoly which the Ballard family had enjoyed since the mid-sixteenth century. Apart from the cumbersome and uneconomic double-impression working, the Ballard monopoly restricted music characters to the outmoded squares and diamonds of the original Le Bé punches. Fournier explained that it seemed fruitless to pursue the ideas for improvement he had been cogitating, since only one person in France was allowed to print music; that was the then reigning Ballard, Christophe-Jean-François, who succeeded his father in 1750 and was summed up by a contemporary as short, fat and lazy—"without much talent".

Breitkopf's 1755 offering of "a new music character, fine and boldly carried out in the style which I had intended to give to mine", Fournier went on, had revived his interest. So he presented the *Essai*—"for which I have been obliged to be the inventor, the cutter, the founder, the compositor and the printer"—in the hope that it "will prove at least that French printing, in assuming this new degree of perfection, will not yield it in any particular to printing in any other part of the world".

The real "new degree of perfection" was in fact only achieved a little later (in 1760), when Fournier produced his much more complicated "second music". This was fully shown in the *Manuel*. Single-impression working was attained by a remarkable unit breakdown of notes and staves so that in appropriate combination an entire score was built up in one piece. The complete music fount comprised 147 consecutively numbered characters (the "bill" totalled 60,000 stamps of type) and clearly the utmost precision was needed in the punch-cutting to secure the smooth and snug joins essential to a pleasant appearance of the printed score.

There were two sizes of the "second music", the *petite musique* and the *grosse musique*. The *petite*, generally thought to be superior to its larger companion, was widely used (it was still in case at the Imprimerie Royale in 1819); it was seen to perfection in a famous song collection, Monnet's *Anthologie Française* of 1765. Fournier cut his music on five different bodies, to cater for the different-sized symbols. As Edmund Poole puts it:

"The minims, crotchets and simple quavers, key signatures, measures and other symbols of the same height were made in one piece (with segments of three or four stave lines incorporated), instead of in the three or four pieces which other systems required. In addition, Fournier provided a wide range of characters which worked with the composite pieces. Fournier claimed that this arrangement made composition simpler, more reliable and quicker. The number of types required was reduced by half: as he says, 'my character being only about 160 matrices instead of at least 300 which other systems carry'." The Fleischman system required 240 matrices, Breitkopf 260 and Rosart 336.

Earlier in this chapter it was noted that Fournier's music-type innovations brought him into collision with the Ballard monopoly interest and into bitter controversy with his competitors the French-Swiss typefounder Nicolas Gando and his son Pierre François, who took it upon themselves to defend the Ballards (no doubt hoping to ingratiate themselves with a family so long so influential in the Paris trade). Gando *père et fils*, who issued a specimen in 1760, were "adroit copyists, and very unscrupulous rivals, of Fournier. . . . And another Gando, François (a brother of Nicolas), first of Lille, later of Paris, also tormented Fournier by his imitations and trickeries";[1] it was Marie Elizabeth, daughter of François Gando, who later married Fournier's nephew Jean François, son of Fournier *l'aîné*, as recorded in chapter 1.

[1] Updike, I p. 271. A notice to printers, issued by Fournier, setting out in parallel columns a number of his types and the Gando plagiarisms has survived inserted in the

C. J. F. Ballard did not scruple to try strong-arm methods when faced with the threat of Fournier's superior music types. From the appearance of the "first music" in the *Essai* in 1756 Fournier had been agitating on what amounted to two fronts—challenging the Ballard music monopoly and claiming the right, as a typefounder, to do his own printing. The wider aspects of this campaign, and the legal actions in which it involved Fournier, are examined in the next chapter. An official decision in Fournier's favour on the music-printing issue was followed by an attempt on Ballard's part to distrain on the new music types in the Fournier foundry (this was in October 1764). Ballard's bailiffs were foiled, it appears, but the incident had a suitably frightening effect on the printer then using the new Fournier music types.[1]

Not surprisingly, Fournier came back at the Ballards in a polemical pamphlet entitled *Traité historique et critique sur l'origine et les progrès des caractères de fonte pour l'impression de la musique* (1765). To this the Ballard-backing Gandos, father and son, retorted with *Observations sur le traité historique* etc (1766) while brother François delivered a side-attack of his own, seeking to defend the Gandos against the design-piracy charge and pretending that the music-printing and music-type issue was a lot of fuss about nothing (he concealed the fact that it was Fournier's agitation which had cleared the way for the court decision of 1764 that any printers might print music—for which, by implication, any founder might cast music-type—while the Ballards retained the privilege of music-printers to the King).

By this time Fournier, deeply engaged on the *Manuel*, and with his *petite musique* adorning Monnet's *Anthologie* (printed by Barbou, his printer), stopped bothering about the Gandos. They toured the south of France trying to rouse printers against him; he disposed of them with a pungent reply to their *Observations* at the end of the second volume of the *Manuel*. Both father and son, he wrote, "had always been nothing but type-founders, never having learnt the art of punchcutting, where their ignorance is total and complete (*pleine et entière*)".[2]

---

copy of the *Modèles* owned by Mme de Langre of Le Mans, a descendant of Fournier (Mosley, p. 19). The Gandos also "lifted" his *Bâtarde Coulée* script—and sold it for 10 per cent less (Warde, p. 28).

[1] Warde, pp. 26, 28.   [2] *Manuel Typographique*, II p. 290.

CHAPTER FIVE

A man of the enlightenment

The two decades that followed the publication of the *Modèles* witnessed both Fournier's establishment as France's leading type-designer and founder and his emergence as a true man of the great Age of Enlightenment (*siècle des lumières*). He was a tireless and lively controversialist, an energetic expositor of the history and practice of the art of printing, a technical innovator of remarkable ingenuity. And parallel with all this, he led a happy and unruffled personal life.

He was 35, and an outstanding figure in the Paris trade, when he married Marie Madeleine Couret de Villeneuve, the sister of a distinguished Orleans printer. By her he had two sons. The elder, Simon Pierre, we have already mentioned as the eventual successor to Fournier's foundry; the younger, Antoine, never had anything to do with the family business and only appears in history much later in an obscure piece of property litigation with his elder brother. The year of his marriage (1747) Fournier left his old home and workshop in the Rue des Sept Voies, opposite the College de Reims, in the heart of the university quarter, to start his family life at the address at the corner of the Place de l'Estrapade and the old Rue des Postes where he was to remain until his death.

The Estrapade-Postes location was still in the university area, not far from the ancient Lycée Henri IV and the picturesque old church of St Etienne du Mont (both still standing) of which Fournier was a parishioner. By all accounts this part of old Paris was then far from being the dark and crowded rookery which one is apt to imagine. No less than one-third of the city was then open land. The streets might be narrow, but there was plenty of space between the houses of one street and the next, with gardens, trees and in general plenty of greenery to delight and comfort the eye. Fournier lived and worked amid "these gardens, these silent streets so propitious to labour, perfumed by lilacs and flowering with pink and white chestnuts". Within this agreeable ambiance, the obituary *éloge* was to say: "Fournier's private life was happy, proving that routine is not always the mother of ennui. His calm spirit diffused about him unruffled and gentle contentment. He fled the noise of society, to enjoy retirement and friendship. . . . Refusing suggested amusement, he devoted himself to work and research".

He was prominent among the scientists, artists and craftsmen who collaborated enthusiastically with Diderot and D'Alembert in the gigantic work of the *Encyclopédie*, whose initial volumes appeared in 1751. This "Descriptive Dictionary of the Sciences, Arts and Crafts", to quote its sub-title, was a unique attempt to synthesise in monumental, and withal living, fashion the whole of human knowledge. The intellectual impact, not only in France, of its 17 massive folio volumes (with 11 volumes of plates) was immense. Nor was it just an exhaustive compendium of information. Its ideological and political implications were profound; not for nothing did a contemporary call it "the holy league against fanaticism and tyranny". All the progressive thinkers of France, the *philosophes*, were there—Voltaire, Rousseau, d'Holbach, Helvetius among many others, including the two editors—and among the technicians whom they welcomed as contributors was the young typefounder of the Rue des Postes.

We do not know how and when Fournier met Diderot and his associates. But the *Discours Préliminaire* written by the master-mathematician D'Alembert for the first volume contained a long list of acknowledgments to experts of all kinds. After thanking Papillon, a famous wood engraver (and a friend of Fournier's) for providing background material "on the history and practice of his art", the next item read "M. Fournier, a very clever typefounder, did the same for typefounding". In effect, the material which Fournier provided must have gone in as the article "Type" (*caractère*) in Vol II. Fournier himself later referred to the "study which I wrote for the *Encyclopédie*" though—in the Introduction to the *Manuel*—he qualified it as "curtailed" and "designed rather for the satisfaction of a reader's curiosity than for the enlightenment of artists".

The article was in fact an impressively detailed one, covering more than ten of the *Encyclopedie*'s vast pages, with an additional three pages of type specimens. Fournier's Table of Proportions was reproduced and explained, fount schemes set forth, the lives of the classic punch-cutters sketched (as in the *Avis* to the *Modèles*). It is charitable to suppose that a number of flattering references to Fournier himself—"clever punch-cutter and founder", "a very competent judge"—may have been subbed in by Diderot. An italic note indicated that all the type specimens came from the foundry of Fournier (i.e. *le jeune*) with the exception only of the *perle* (4pt) and the *Parisienne* (5pt), provided by the Imprimerie Royale. Since the largest sizes shown were Le Bé types from the foundry of Fournier *l'aîné*, as in the *Modèles*, the lack of any acknowledgment here was to provoke a public complaint in the press from the elder brother.[1] The *Encyclopédie* specimens show the 1749 size of the *Bâtarde Coulée* script, despite Fournier's own curious claim, quoted in chapter 3, that he did not provide the two sizes of this letter until 1752.

In his enthusiasm for exposition and polemic—they can hardly be separated—Fournier was entirely at one with his age in general, and his friends the *Encyclopédistes*. He contributed pieces of information or controversy to contemporary journals like the *Observations sur les Ecrits Modernes*, the *Journal des Savants*, the *Mercure de France*. The success of the *Modèles* early embroiled him with some of his trade confrères, like Luce and Lamesle (not to mention the Gandos); like the "wicked animal" of the French adage, when he was attacked he defended himself. To the charge that he had imitated Grandjean and Alexandre's italics he coolly replied "If altering, correcting, giving new outlines is inventing, then I invented these letters", going on to detail the differences in drawing which made significant changes and improvements. It seems peculiar that Stanley Morison should have thought this "not candid".[2]

There was something of the Voltairian *écrasez l'infâme* about Fournier's spirited onslaught on anomalies like the music monopoly of the Ballard family (as discussed in chapter 4) and the support of the Ballards by the piratical Gandos. His contemptuous dismissal of the Gandos and their "total and complete ignorance" has already been quoted. He came at them again when François Gando, younger brother of Nicolas (head of

[1] Mosley, p. 14.

[2] Carter, p. 290n: Stanley Morison, *A Tally of Types* (Cambridge, 1953), p. 61.

the Gando firm), flooded Paris printshops with a sheet showing genuine Fournier italics, together with the Gando copies and the impudent caption "It can be seen at first glance how I have succeeded in imitating the new italics cut by Fournier *le jeune*". Fournier curtly signalled the obvious defects of the pirated founts and put François *le jeune* in his place with the chill phrase that "his meagre talents have relegated him to a town in Flanders".[1]

Fournier was addicted to "Historical and Critical Treatises" on all aspects of printing and its origins. We have already referred to his *Traité Historique et Critique* of 1765 on music type and the Ballard monopoly. Under a similar general title Barbou presented in one elegant 8vo volume of more than 500 pages five separate works published at various dates between 1758 and 1763; they showed Fournier's type—including the decorated capitals and the script—and ornaments, and Barbou's setting and presswork at their best. No. 1 dealt with early wood-engraving, No. 2 with early block-books and printing with wood letter (both aimed to show that Gutenberg was not the true inventor of printing), No. 3 tackled Professor Schoepflin of Strasbourg (who sought to establish the primacy of that city as the birthplace of printing and appeared to lean towards the claim that Laurens Coster of Haarlem antedated Gutenberg), No. 4 roughly took to task a Swedish scholar, the Rev Charles Baer (who had rushed to Schoepflin's defence), No. 5 was a neat bibliographical demolition of a supposedly earliest-printed Bible.

Though he was anti-Gutenberg, Fournier was not pro-Coster (whose claim he thought merely due to "national prejudice"). In general, he firmly argued that only someone with all-round printing experience could seriously discuss the origin of printing, acidly concluding—à propos the Rev Charles Baer—"devoid of any knowledge of the history and practice of printing, this author fails to provide a single thought, a single story, a single notion, which could be of the least utility".[2]

More than two centuries later it is easy to pick holes in Fournier's scholarship, much of which we may feel to be more antiquarian than scientific. Nevertheless Morison's characterisation of Fournier as an "egoist" who was "better artist than scholar" seems somewhat patronising.

[1] Fournier, *Avis Particulier de l'Auteur* (*Dissertation*, etc, 1758, pp. 87-92).
[2] Fournier, *Remarques*, etc (1761), p. 84.

Fournier's scholarship has to be judged in his own, eighteenth century, terms; and as a statement of scholarly attitude no fault can surely be found with his declaration "I will examine everything with the care and exactness of an artist who has no aim other than the truth".[1]

The men of the Enlightenment had wide horizons. Their attitude was the reverse of parochial. French scholarship was international. Leading *Encyclopédistes* were proud to count themselves members of the Royal Academies of Prussia or Fellows of the Royal Society. Fournier entirely shared this wide world outlook. In 1756 he contributed a survey of contemporary printing to the *Journal des Savants*; percipiently he gave high praise to the bookwork of Robert and Andrew Foulis, the brothers who were printers to the University of Glasgow, whose original typography might well have been thought hardly to have penetrated beyond these islands. It is worth noting that, like Fournier's own types, those used by the Foulis brothers were "transitionals"; they came from Alexander Wilson, who in 1742 had started Scotland's first typefoundry and whose letter-design in the 1750s was much influenced by Baskerville.

In this same article, with a certain historic irony, Fournier discharged a broadside at his Dutch contemporaries for their money-making passion to save space, which "has led them deliberately to acquire types of a cramped, starved look, so that they may get in more words to the line and more lines to the page. They are not troubled by their ugliness, provided they are profitable". This at once contrasted with his later praise of Fleischman, the first cutter of these big-on-the-body, condensed faces (as mentioned in chapter 2) and the fact that he himself was about to offer "Dutch style" as one of the variants in several of his sizes.[2]

By this time Fournier's European standing was such that he was asked to advise on the setting-up of Royal printing-houses for Sweden and Sardinia; he sold strikes to both countries. And here, perhaps, it will be suitable to mention the survey of European typefoundries which he presented in Volume II of the *Manuel*. Factually, as Harry Carter has remarked, it was defective and often wildly out of date; nevertheless it was truly a "pioneer work". The section on France was naturally well-

[1] Morison, ibid: Fournier, *De l'Origine et des Productions de l'Imprimerie Primitive*, etc (1759), p. 8.

[2] Carter, pp. xxii, 272n.

informed but those on Holland, Germany, England, Italy, Spain and the Scandinavian countries had many errors and omissions. He thought that Thomas Cottrell (the craftsman whom Caslon sacked in 1757 for organising a strike, and thereafter started his own London foundry which eventually descended to the present Stephenson Blake concern) was at Oxford and mentioned James Watson of Edinburgh (Watson was not a founder at all, but a printer who used imported Dutch type; in 1713 he wrote *The History of the Art of Printing*). However, he praised William Caslon and John Baskerville as "worthy of special attention" and continued with a panegyric of Birmingham's "eccentric amateur" (as Breitkopf called him), whose types "are cut with great daring, and the italic is the best to be found in any English foundry". Baskerville's books were "veritable masterpieces of clarity" and their hot-pressed glossy paper made them "the finest thing yet seen of their kind".[1]

Fournier interestingly included Russia in his survey; his friend Breit-kopf would no doubt have provided him with information, since the Leipzig founders had long cultivated the Russian market. This may account for the fact that, though he was inaccurate, he was (if it may be put that way) not too inaccurate. He was wrong in saying that Russia had had no typefoundries until around 1750; the press of the Academy of Sciences in Petersburg had its own typefoundry long before that, issuing important specimen books in 1744 and 1748, though the press of Moscow University did not get a foundry until some time later. Fournier then indicated that both establishments had, at or about the date suggested, bought strikes from Leipzig and Wittenberg; in fact it was the Moscow press which imported its roman type from foundries in these German centres, getting its Russian type from the Academy's foundry in Petersburg. When Fournier, however, concluded that "since then a tolerably skilful letter-cutter has moved to St Petersburg, where he has cut letter of several kinds" he may well have been correctly informed. Forty years ago Harry Carter was unable to trace this Petersburg cutter; but from modern Soviet scholarship in the printing historical field it may be deduced that the cutter was Ivan Sokolov, chief foreman-engraver of the engraving and punch-cutting department at the typefoundry of the Academy of Sciences; there were five foremen-engravers, 15 assistants and 30 apprentices. Sokolov

[1] Carter, pp. xxxi, 274–6.

had been actively cutting punches in Petersburg since the 1740s.[1]

This chapter began by saying that Fournier was a technical innovator of remarkable ingenuity as well as an indefatigable polemicist and expositor. His innovations varied both in kind and in degree. We have already had occasion to notice some of them—his point system, his new-style italics, his music-type, his flowers, his variant faces, his metal poster types. These may reasonably be called his typographic innovations; but he was also an innovator in the sheer mechanics of typefounding. Thus his ability to offer rules (and leads) up to the then remarkable length of 14 inches resulted from his invention of moulds for the "continuous" casting of rules and leads. To the detailed description of these moulds and the mode of their operation he devoted chapters XXX and XXXI of the *Manuel*. These have a curiously modern ring; all we have done this century is to mechanise our continuous lead and rule casting, with machines like the Monotype Super-Caster, the Elrod and other strip casters; and the length of the product has been increased to 24 inches.

With equal ingenuity Fournier tackled the problem of badly-cut or warped wood furniture, which had long tended to cause trouble when trueing-up a forme of type. The answer, he saw, lay in metal furniture; so in 1763 he devised a special mould for the purpose, with a sliding bottom to control the length and breadth of the furniture cast. The larger sizes could be hollowed out (*Manuel*, chapter XXXII). So it was that printers in this country came to call metal furniture "French furniture" ("originally a French idea"—i.e. an idea of Fournier's—as Charles T. Jacobi's *Printers' Vocabulary* put it in 1888).

As a corollary of Fournier's fixing of type bodies and proportionate relations by his point system he invented a "universal pattern for the body and height-to-paper of letters" (*Manuel*, chapter XXVIII). This, of which he was very proud, he called the "prototype". He described it as a "new instrument, made of iron and copper", measuring exactly 240pts; thus it would take 40 *nompareilles* or 20 *cicéros* to fill it. In this way the accuracy of a given casting of a given size could be checked in the same instrument, instead of in a rough-and-ready lining-stick made up for a particular fount. The "prototype", Fournier emphasised, "produces a degree of

[1] Carter, pp. 279–81: A. G. Shitsgal, *Russky Grazhdansky Shrift* (Moscow 1959) pp. 119, 126.

precision not heretofore attained" and he thought that such an instrument might well be deposited with the *chambre syndicale* of Paris printers "to serve as a legal standard. This would be a sure, convenient, and unerring method of ensuring type against dangerous variations".

The "prototype" checked the accuracy of the castings, particularly it seems if the mould was casting fractionally too large; for Fournier added that the type-dresser "does the rest by paring the letters to the required extent until the given number exactly fills the length of the instrument". The trouble was that Fournier's point system depended on a printed scale of two inches, divided into 144pts, and (as he admitted) the shrinkage that followed printing on damped paper could produce slight, but significant, variations. Noting this Updike added that the "prototype" itself "was probably subject to slight variations in manufacture, and was in no sense an instrument of precision". True; but Fournier's procedure was certainly more precise, however relative that might be, than anything that had gone before.[1]

Finally, Fournier devoted great attention to the dressing-block (*Manuel*, chapter XXXIII), the instrument which put the final touches to the cast type by planing the feet even. The dressing-block, or bench, had traditionally been of wood, though Jean Jannon of Sedan had devised an iron block in 1630, which had evidently not caught on among typefounders. Pierre Cot in Paris had revived it around 1700 but, Fournier continues, "it was owing to my labours that it was brought, in 1739, to the state in which I describe it". The description is very long and very technical. What is notable is that Fournier stressed its value, not only for increasing output, but for contributing to the "comfort of the workman". The old-fashioned wooden blocks, for instance, had their adjusting screw so positioned that the dresser was "obliged to lean his body over seven or eight hundred times a day", while a projecting portion of the block "hits him in the stomach each time". But with Fournier's block "the man works in a natural posture, with greater ease".

Fournier's battle over music-type and music-printing, which the previous chapter discussed, showed him in the combined role of innovator and polemicist. As already said, this fight soon embraced a wider issue than the music question. For Fournier, with his unitary conception of the

[1] Updike, I p. 31.

design, manufacture and use of type, it was intolerably frustrating to be debarred, by the legally-enforced monopoly of the Parisian master printers, from owning a press or printing, even for his own private use. In January 1757 he addressed a formal petition to *Monseigneur le Chancelier* for a legal ruling compelling the *chambre syndicale* to admit him as a master printer without undergoing the requisite apprenticeship (which required that candidates should be unmarried and also conversant with Latin and Greek). He was especially anxious to be able to print himself the *Manuel Typographique*.

The opposition, Ballard-led, delivered a slashing attack on Fournier's claims, asserting that his work was imitative, that his music-type was inferior to Breitkopf's and that he may have sold type "to secret presses consecrated to blasphemy and irreligion". The case lingered on for years, but in 1762 went in Fournier's favour. An Order in Council decreed his admission as "supernumerary printer for the City of Paris", with the added privilege of "printing works of music of any kind". This additional clause gave Ballard his pretext to rouse his cronies in the leadership of the master printers to get the Order nullified; they were able to do this because they were on good terms with the Chief of Police, De Sartine, who had power to suspend the operation of Orders of this sort. Thus, by a piece of sharp practice, Fournier was foiled of his victory on the broad issue of a type-founder's right to print, though he had managed to breach the Ballard music monopoly.[1]

[1] Carter, pp. xxvi–xxix: Warde, pp. 35-36.

CHAPTER SIX

The crowning of a career

Fournier's *Manuel Typographique* crowned his career. We have seen how, in addition to his astonishing one-man performance as type-designer, punch-cutter and founder (not to mention setting and making-up his own specimen pages), he was a tireless controversialist particularly in matters of printing history, and an enthusiastic expositor of the practical aspects of the printing art. All this was leading up to the great work he had planned for many years and which, as its title showed, was to embrace the whole of typography in that term's widest possible sense. It was to have been in four volumes: I) Type, its cutting and founding, II) Printing and its techniques, III) The lives and work of the great "typographers" (defined by Fournier as those with the triple mastery of punch-cutting, typefounding and printing), IV) Type specimens, including examples of exotic alphabets.[1]

Unhappily, Fournier only lived to complete the first and fourth volumes, the last of which in the event was published as Vol II (it included the survey of foreign typefoundries already mentioned in the previous chapter). So the title is by way of being a misnomer; and what we have is a torso, not the total monument. But what a torso! Even Updike, whose attitude to Fournier was always marked by a certain ambivalence, wrote that "the simplicity of the author's style, his naive pride in his own performances, and its mass of information make a book which will become a favourite with anyone who reads it. It is not the work of a scholar, but of an observing, experienced, quick-witted master of his art, who in cultivating that art had cultivated himself".[2]

[1] F. Thibaudeau, *La Lettre d'Imprimerie*, I p. 300: Carter, p. 14.
[2] Updike, I p. 265.

We have seen how Fournier's battle to break the music-printing mono-poly widened into a demand for his right as typefounder to print, for his own purposes and not by way of competitive trade; it will be recalled that it was, the *Manuel* he had in mind. Before the first volume appeared there was the usual prolonged pre-revolutionary procedure to secure the Royal *privilège* and its subsequent registration with the *chambre syndicale* of the Paris master-printers. This took from 1761 to 1763—just straddling the year when Fournier finally got his abortive permission to function as a "supernumerary printer" for the City of Paris; the final endorsement was signed by the then *syndic* of the master-printers, Le Breton, printer (and eventually saboteur) of the *Encyclopédie*. Updike seems to have thought that the permission of 1762 enabled Fournier to print the *Manuel* himself, ignoring the fact that the master-printers' action, recorded in chapter 5, had rendered it null and void. Fournier evidently had some provisional concession from the authorities, however; for when Vol I was published, in 1764, its title-page bore the legend "Printed by the Author and sold by Barbou" (the printer). But this did not survive. Vol II bore Barbou's imprint with the indication that the book could be "had from the Author" (*chez l'auteur*).[1]

As production pieces both volumes of the *Manuel* were models of Fournier's art. In pocket-sized, 16mo format (French writers often use the term "small octavo") they were gay with decoration, all pages bordered, the introductions (*avertissements préliminaires*) set in *cicéro ordinaire*, well-leaded, with the text of Vol I in the condensed *poétique* of the same size. Vol II's comments on the 101 alphabets shown after the type specimens were set down a size—to *philosophie* (11pt) *poétique*. A note at the end of Vol II explained that, though it was dated 1766 (the year it was intended to publish) the publication had been delayed until 1768 "due to the author's long illness"; Fournier was to die later that year. A further note stated that a few copies of the *Manuel* had been produced on "glazed paper" (no doubt emulating the already much-admired hot-pressing of "M. Basker-ville of Birmingham"); it is not clear whether these copies bear any rela-tion to the "copies on large paper" which Bigmore and Wyman, in their note on the *Manuel*, described as "of the greatest rarity".[2]

[1] Updike, I p. 261n.
[2] *Manuel*, II p. 288: Bigmore and Wyman, *Bibliography of Printing* (1884), I p. 228.

The *Manuel* set its own note with its sub-title—"Useful to men of letters and to those who are practitioners in the different branches of the Art of Printing". Allowing for a certain untranslatable quality in the French *gens de lettres* ("literary men" may perhaps be somewhat nearer) it is clear that Fournier was aiming at the *cognoscenti*, both on the literary and the technical sides. He was not producing a primer for the aspiring apprentice or the young journeyman, as Fertel had already done in his *Science Pratique*; on the other hand he much admired Fertel's manual—"and as he did not fear to say, he was largely inspired by the work of this author in his own presentation".[1] As it happened, of course, all Fournier's basic writing in the *Manuel* (Vol I) was entirely concerned with type and type-founding. He thought, and said, that he was first in the field in the description of the processes of punch-cutting and the details of type manufacture. His French insularity evidently accounted for his being unaware of his English and German predecessors. Joseph Moxon's famous account of type-cutting and casting, the *Mechanick Exercises,* London-published in 1683, had been followed nearer Fournier's own day by *Kurze doch Nützliche Anleitung von Form- und Stahl-Schneiden* (Erfurt, 1754).

However, Fournier's claim to primacy was fair enough in respect of France; as he said of his type-designing, punchcutting compatriots, "none has dealt in writing with the practice of his art; for which reason, when I wished to master it I was obliged to establish principles for myself and to lay down my own rules: these I shall state in the succeeding part of this work". Describing typography as "the art of all arts and the science of all sciences", through which men were provided with "a means of mutually communicating their enlightenment", he observed that it was "greatly to be wished that every literary man were in a position to form a sound judgment upon the typography of his books" which would in turn mean

---

The *Manuel* has always been a rare work and now fetches a very high price. In 1928 the Birrell and Garnett *Typefounders' Specimens* catalogue offered a copy at 15gns; in 1970 a copy was sold in New York for the equivalent of £300, and an expert bookselling view is that, according to condition, the price here would now range from £250 to £400; in 1942, with the antiquarian bookselling business at its wartime rock bottom, the late Irving Davis, senior partner of Davis and Orioli, offered me a fine copy for £5 —and I had no fiver to spare (or so I thought)!

[1] Thibaudeau, *op. cit.,* I p. 269.

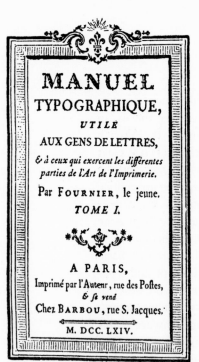

MANUEL
TYPOGRAPHIQUE,
UTILE
AUX GENS DE LETTRES,
*& à ceux qui exercent les différentes
parties de l'Art de l'Imprimerie.*
Par FOURNIER, le jeune.
TOME I.

A PARIS,
Imprimé par l'Auteur, rue des Postes,
& se vend
Chez BARBOU, rue S. Jacques.
M. DCC. LXIV.

MANUEL
TYPOGRAPHIQUE.

PREMIÈRE PARTIE.

LA GRAVURE,
OU TAILLE DES POINÇONS.

POUR être un bon Graveur de Caractères, il faut être Typographe, c'est-à-dire, savoir tous les détails du méchanisme de la Fonderie & de l'Imprimerie, afin d'y assujétir son travail. Maître de l'art, le Graveur doit tout prévoir dans la fonte & dans l'impression. C'est par-là que les Simon de Colines, les Garamond, les

A

CICÉRO POÉTIQUE.

UN Général d'armée recevant de toutes parts des plaintes contre un Munitionnaire, le fit venir, & pour premier compliment le menaça de le faire pendre. Monseigneur, répondit froidement le Munitionnaire, on ne pend pas quelqu'un qui peut disposer de cent mille écus; & là-dessus ils passerent dans le cabinet. Un instant après, Monsieur le Général en sortit persuadé que c'étoit un fort honnête-homme.

Ceci nous apprend qu'on ne doit pas juger trop précipitamment de la conduite du prochain, ni le condamner sans l'entendre. Il est bien aisé de dire que certaines gens sont des fripons, mais il faut le prouver.

CICÉRO POÉTIQUE.

VOUS avez une pièce d'argent, ou même une pièce d'or, ce n'est pas assez; c'est le nombre qui opère; faites-en, si vous pouvez, un amas considérable & qui s'élève en pyramide, & je me charge du reste. Vous n'avez ni connoissances, ni esprit, ni talens, ni expérience; n'importe: ne diminuez rien de votre monceau, & je vous placerai si haut, que vous vous couvrirez devant votre maître, si vous en avez: il sera même fort éminent, si avec votre métal qui de jour à autre se multiplie, je ne fais en sorte qu'il se découvre devant vous.

La plupart des gens ne jugent des hommes que par la vogue qu'ils ont, ou par leur fortune.

CICÉRO, PETIT ŒIL.

LE Directeur à la mode, semblable au Médecin, flatte, console, encourage, entretient la délicatesse & la sensibilité sur soi-même; il n'ordonne que de petits remèdes benins, & qui se tournent en habitude. On ne fait que tournoyer dans un petit cercle de vertus communes, au-delà desquelles on ne passe jamais généreusement.

Certains Dévots n'aiment jamais tant Dieu que lorsqu'ils ont obtenu leurs satisfactions temporelles; ils ne prient jamais mieux que quand l'esprit & la chair sont contens & qu'ils prient ensemble.

CICÉRO SERRÉ.

LES inférieurs, avec un respect bien attentif & bien sérieux, sont quittes de ce qu'ils doivent aux Grands, lorsque ces Grands n'ont pas d'autre mérite que les Grades ou les Dignités qui les distinguent des autres hommes. Combien la supériorité de ceux-là est peu digne d'envie, quand elle ne leur rapporte que le seul tribut que l'usage demande!

Respecter scrupuleusement les Grands, sans avoir d'autres sentimens pour eux, c'est mettre à part leur personne, & ne rendre hommage & honneur qu'à leur destinée: c'est n'entretenir une Divinité que de la beauté du piédestal qui l'élève.

Title and opening pages of the Manuel Typographique *(all reduced)*

CICÉRO ORDINAIRE.

L'AIR que nous refpirons, nos alimens, les faifons, le climat, le tempérament, l'âge, l'extraction même, & ces difpofitions intérieures au bien & au mal que le fang des pères communique à leurs enfans, font autant d'ennemis qui attaquent notre raifon & nos fens, & qui corrompent notre jugement.

L'habitude non feulement adoucit les difgraces de notre condition préfente, mais encore elle femble changer la qualité des chofes auxquelles nous nous accoûtumons.

On doit autant à l'habitude qu'à la raifon.

CICÉRO, ŒIL MOYEN.

VEUT-ON infpirer aux enfans, nés dans un rang fupérieur ou dans un état diftingué, les qualités qu'ils doivent apporter dans la fociété? On doit s'attacher fans ceffe à ne leur faire envifager la grandeur, que par ce qu'elle a de facile, de doux & de careffant; que par les bienfaits qu'elle peut procurer ou répandre; ne leur peindre la fortune que fous les traits de libéralité; n'appeler enfin devant eux tous les avantages qu'ils poffèdent, que du nom des vertus qui en peuvent naître, ou du bien qui en réfulte.

CICÉRO, GROS ŒIL.

L'AMOUR eft une paffion de l'appétit concupifcible qui fe porte au bien fenfible, conçu tel par l'imagination, & l'amitié eft une vertu qui porte notre volonté au bien honnête, conçu tel par l'entendement. Le premier eft fouvent contraire à l'autre, car les paffions violentes troublent la raifon, & l'excès d'amour dégénère en jaloufie; au lieu que l'amitié ne peut avoir d'excès, & qu'elle mérite d'autant mieux le nom d'amitié, qu'elle eft étendue, & même extrême.

CICÉRO ORDINAIRE.

BON nombre de fils de famille marqués de quelques défauts effentiels, font ornés d'un petit collet: il eft bien peu d'enfans de Gentilshommes, & même de Bourgeois, lorfqu'ils font difgraciés de la Nature, qui ne foient confacrés au fervice des Autels. Quelle vocation!

Les défauts corporels ne font cependant pas des marques de ceux de l'ame; la plus belle & la plus grande eft fouvent logée dans le corps le plus contrefait & le plus difforme. L'illuftre Prince de Condé & le fameux Maréchal de Luxembourg, chacun d'une figure defagréable, furent néanmoins des Héros.

CICÉRO, GROS ŒIL,
dans le goût Hollandois.

LA pluspart des hommes de Lettres ne fe piquent que de doctrine & d'érudition; ils entaffent livres fur livres, fcience fur fcience qui ne produifent que de l'obfcurité, de la féchereffe & du travers dans l'efprit: c'eft pourquoi il fe trouve plus de gens de favoir que de bon fens.

Le bon fens va droit au vrai; l'éloquence n'en eft que l'interprète, & tout fon but eft de lui donner de la force & de la clarté: fi quelquefois elle s'échappe à y jeter de certains agrémens, c'eft pour le rendre plus aimable.

CICÉRO, GROS ŒIL.

LA dernière chofe où l'on s'applique, c'eft à épurer fon difcernement: on exerce fa raifon à toutes fortes d'études qui ne fervent qu'à l'embarraffer, au lieu qu'il ne faut étudier que pour inftruire & perfectionner fa raifon.

On peut dire que les femmes qui ne s'occupent point de fciences & de littérature, confervent plus que les hommes la tranquillité de l'ame: la frivolité de leurs occupations leur tient ordinairement l'efprit libre & le rend plus aimable.

The Manuel's *full range of* cicéro *(12pt) specimens: see p. 65 below*

that printers "would be obliged to have sufficient respect for his work not to disfigure it, as they so often do, with the results of their ignorance and want of taste". Thus his double aim in the *Manuel* was "to give scholars a conception of the art of typography, and at the same time to recall to its practitioners certain principles of which they should be aware".

His own exacting criterion was expressed in the definition of typography as "consisting of three parts, each distinct and indispensable, namely, punchcutting, founding and printing. The practice of the different branches produces artists of three different kinds, the first punchcutters, the second founders, and the third printers, but only he who combines a knowledge of all three branches is fit to be styled a TYPOGRAPHER. There have been few artists of the first kind, rather more of the second, many of the third, and extremely few of the fourth: those, I mean, who have earned the name of typographer". Here Fournier unconsciously echoed Moxon: "By a Typographer I do not mean a Printer, as he is Vulgarly accounted. . . . I mean such a one, who by his own Judgment, from solid reasoning with himself, can either perform, or direct others to perform from the beginning to the end, all the Handy-works and Physical Operations relating to Typographie".[1]

Moxon was able to achieve what Fournier unfortunately was not; namely to cover printing (composition and presswork) as well as punchcutting and typefounding. A comparison of the 40-odd sections of the *Mechanick Exercises* describing "letter-cutting", moulds, matrix-striking, type-metal, the casting and final processing ("dressing") of type, with Fournier's 36 chapters, show how much common ground there was between them. The basic techniques had not changed between the late seventeenth and the middle eighteenth century. Fournier's exposition was, as we might now say, more sophisticated; his 16 double-page copperplate engravings exceeded Moxon's crude illustrations in precision and elegance; and his end-product was much superior, as a glance at his and Moxon's type-specimens instantly shows.

The first ten chapters of the *Manuel* expound punchcutting, in general and in particular; the next two discuss matrix-making; typefounding, again in general and in particular, occupies 16 chapters—including one

[1] Carter, pp. 1-4, 12-14: Joseph Moxon, *Mechanick Exercises* (edited by Herbert Davis and Harry Carter, Oxford, 1958), pp. 11-12.

on Fournier's final point system (dealt with separately below) and on his invention of the "prototype" gauge for checking overall accuracy of casting (discussed in chapter 5); six chapters are devoted to the different sorts of mould, the caster's furnace and the dressing-block (Fournier's innovations in this important equipment have likewise been treated in the previous chapter); the next chapter goes into great detail on the vital matter of fount schemes; a concluding chapter, hardly more than a paragraph, is headed "Typography"—it makes the point that while printing is but the "third part" of the art "it is the part to which the others owe their existence" and therefore "consummates the work"; it would therefore be the subject of the *Manuel's* (never to appear) third volume.[1]

Right at the start of his first chapter, "Punchcutting: General Principles", Fournier reiterated his unitary concept of typography in these words: "A man cannot be a good punchcutter without being a typographer, that is to say he must know every detail of the operations involved in typefounding and printing, that he may work with an eye to them. Holding as it were the key to the whole of the art, the punchcutter should anticipate every step in the casting and impression of the letters. . . . It is, perhaps, possible to be a good punchcutter without practising printing, but not without understanding the theory of it". The art of the punchcutter was "to know the best possible shape that can be given to letters, and their proper relation to one another, and to be able to reproduce them upon steel so that they may be struck into copper to make the matrices by means of which the letters can ever after be cast in any numbers".[2]

Determination of the subtle relationship between the x-height (the "short" letters), the ascenders, descenders and those letters occupying the full depth of the body, was the subject of Chapter II, "The Face-Gauge". Fournier divided the body depth into seven equal parts, allowing three for the x-height and five for ascending or descending letters. These depths were notched in a small piece of thin brass, roman one side, italic (with certain modifications) the other. These gauges guided the punchcutter. Chapter III, "Punches and Counter-punches", threw much light on the complexity and delicacy of his task. The counter-punch, giving the shape

[1] Carter, pp. ix–x, 245.
[2] Carter, pp. 20ff. All subsequent quotations from the *Manuel* in this chapter are from the indicated chapters in the Carter translation.

of the inside (the "counter") of the particular letter or letters—some counter-punches served for several letters—was cut and hardened first. The counter-punch was then struck into the squared end of a two-inch steel bar, suitably softened by annealing (Fournier discoursed in some detail on modes of annealing steel). The cutter then set to work on the outside of the letter with files of varying degrees of fineness. Fournier argued over the suitable depth of the counters—the Dutch, he thought, went too deep—and outlined the processes for the smooth finishing of the punch, together with the checking of its progress by means of smoke proofs.

Chapters IV and V told how the above procedures, applying to body sizes, had to be modified for the larger display letters (where the cold chisel and the twist-drill were called upon) and for flowers, whose elaborate counters had to be cut out with gravers, and which required special care in cutting so that they would be flush with their body and thus join smoothly in combination. Fournier described an ingenious way of reversing flowers by taking an impression from a finished punch on the waxed end of a punch bar.

The peculiar and complicated features of music-type cutting were the subject of Chapters VI–IX inclusive; their interest, to put it plainly, is esoteric, though the first two—dealing with plain-chant notes and staves for church hymnals—testified to Fournier's virtuosity in this obscure field (he described a method he had devised for improvements in the style of notes for red-and-black plain-chant, of which Vol II of the *Manuel* contained a folding-sheet specimen). Chapter IX, "Cutting the New Music", gave the technical details of Fournier's 160-punch music-type system, and included some points of controversy on this somewhat explosive issue, of which chapter 4 has already treated.

Chapters X–XII were devoted to the hardening and tempering of the punch, the striking and justifying of the copper matrices. Typefounders were later to employ a screw-operated device to drive the vertically-accurate punch into the matrix, with a gauge to indicate the depth of strike. Fournier described the primitive method of his day, whereby the punch "is beaten in with a hammer as perpendicularly as possible"; he evidently was aware of the problem of accurate striking under these conditions, for he added that this operation "is forthwith repeated with several punches, whereby the hand gains experience and the strikes

become increasingly level". Again he dwelt on the different treatments required for large display types; either the copper matrix had to be heated or,
in the case of the monster poster types for which Fournier was famous,
chisel-cutting had to be combined with slow and gradual punch-striking.
The "justification" of the matrix, namely its trueing-up and careful checking for depth of strike (which determined the height-to-paper of the
ultimate casting), proper set and alignment, was expounded in detail; and
with a nice, homely touch Fournier told how, after the punches had struck
their matrices, the punch-cutter "lovingly ties them in a bundle, and to
preserve them and shield them from rust . . . he gives them a light coat-
ing of olive-oil, and stores them in a dry place".

Punches and matrices thus disposed of, the remaining chapters turned
to the actual typefounding. In Chapter XIII, discussing the general
principles of founding, Fournier noted the then usual range of 20 type
sizes (*Parisienne* or 5pt to *grosse nompareille* or 96pt). Commenting further
on the face variants of the same body, which will be referred to in more
detail in the next chapter, dealing with Vol II of the *Manuel*, he concluded
that with some allowance for exotics, music, two-line titlings and flowers a
typefoundry needed a stock of at least 20,000 matrices. Chapter XIV, "A
General View of Letter-Founding", presented a vivid picture of type
manufacture in its unmechanised days. Holding the matrix-holding mould
in his left hand the caster ladled in molten metal, giving a peculiar jerk
(the "caster's shake") to drive the metal well into the matrix. The mould
itself—described in Chapter XXIX—consisted of two wooden halves,
closed by a spring, and embodying some 50 iron parts, including the necessary screws and nuts, and with the "bodies" which controlled the size
being cast. Fournier stressed the constant vigilance, indeed procedure
by trial and error, called for during casting; it is not surprising that his
estimate of output per caster was no more than 2–3,000 types a day. After
the breaking off of the projecting "jet" left by the casting, there followed
the finishing operations (Chapters XXXIII "The Dressing Block") and
the checking for accuracy (Chapter XXVIII "The Prototype"). Finally
the type, "having already passed through eight or ten hands" was packeted
in "pages" weighing 8–9lb for dispatch to the printer-customer.

In Chapters XVIII to XXVII Fournier then expatiated on various details
of the general picture—the determination of height-to-paper, alignment

and set, the "nick" (the mark on the shank of the letter which indicates whether it is right way up), two-line titlings, flowers and ornaments, leads, fractions, music. Chapters XXX to XXXII described the continuous lead and rule, and metal furniture, moulds, which were Fournier's own invention and which the preceding chapter has touched on. Even the clay-built caster's furnace attracted Fournier's practical attention; in Chapter XXXIV he explained how he had fitted the furnace mouth with a sheet-iron door "which makes this furnace safer from accidents with fire, and cleaner and more convenient".

Typefounding cannot be discussed without some consideration of type-metal. Fournier did this in masterly and novel fashion in his Chapters XV and XVI. Tin had not then found its way into the type-metal formula as the toughener that we consider essential. The old founders simply used antimony to harden their lead; but traditionally they had employed crude antimony, in the form of stibnite, a natural sulphide of antimony. When stibnite was heated with pieces of scrap iron—it was quite erroneously believed that old horseshoe nails were the best for this purpose—metallic antimony was released and iron sulphide formed. Performing this operation with lead to produce type-metal resulted in a great deal of dross and an unsatisfactory alloy. Fournier realised that metallic antimony—the "regulus"—must be produced first and then melted, in the right proportions, with lead to make a sound type-metal. He found that the regulus of antimony was scarce and dear, so he studied the metallurgy of the business (as Chapter XVI shows in considerable detail), got smelting plants set up at Orleans and elsewhere, "with the result that through my efforts it has become more widely used and obtainable at a more reasonable rate".

Reguline antimony, Fournier claimed, "causes no hurt to our workmen" contrary to the "too common prejudice which causes antimony to be regarded as a poison". Moxon—who was certainly using stibnite, not the regulus—mentioned the custom by which "Half a Pint of Sack mingled with Sallad Oyl [is] for each Workman to Drink; intended for an Antidote against the Poysonous Fumes of the *Antimony*".[1]

Mention has already been made of the elegant engravings which illustrate Vol I. They are at once precise and detailed and can be seen, excellently reproduced, in Harry Carter's 1930 translation, so often quoted in

[1] Moxon, *op. cit.*, p. 167.

these pages. Fournier's explanatory notes, with numbered references to the items, make them fully comprehensible. Plate I (the furnace for making type-metal) shows 12 items, Plate II (the caster's furnace) nine, Plates III and IV (instruments for punchcutting) no fewer than 33, including gauges, punches and counter-punches, files and other tools, Plates V and VI (the letter-mould) have together 25 items on this central piece of equipment, while Plate VII (mould used in Germany and Holland) has 12. Plate VIII shows ten items, including the famous Prototype and other gauges, together with space and quad matrices and such an incidental instrument as the knife for clearing "kerns" (the overhang of lower-case "f", for instance). Plates IX and X (moulds for rules, leads, metal furniture) total 40 items. Plates XI covered Fournier's invention of the iron dressing-block in 17 items, while Plate XIII disposed of the old-fashioned wooden dressing-block with eight (one of these being "mallet"). Plate XII (dressing-planes) exhibited these instruments, with their various irons, in 15 items, while the remaining three plates (XIV–XVI) showed 25 miscellaneous items of equipment, ranging from saws and grindstones to a cupboard for storing punches and matrices.

Two important chapters in Vol I, certainly part of the work but with their own distinct interest, now call for concluding mention. Chapter XXXV, on fount schemes (*police*) accompanied by detailed tables of the different schemes, testified once again to Fournier's high degree of practicality. He argued that ordering founts by weight was the most economical procedure; to order by the sheet or by the case, as some printers did, was bound to be wasteful. He gave the weights in French *livres* (slightly less than the English pound) for 1,000 and 100,000 letters of the main type sizes; the 100,000 fount of *nompareille* weighed 100 *livres*, that of *cicéro* 325. Quads and spaces were additional, at the rate of 10 per cent of the weight of type.

Fournier explained how his fount schemes were based on a calculation of letter-occurrence in sample pages of print or manuscript; he prudently noted that if the fount were required for setting Latin the numbers of certain letters, and the diphthong "ae", must be substantially increased over the scheme for French. Special schemes were presented for Hebrew, Greek (of extreme complexity), his *caractère de finance* with its many additional sorts, and for music (the 147 characters on five different bodies were consecutively numbered for reference, and corresponding spaces for various note widths added). His standard roman fount of 100,000 letters included, in addition to caps and small caps, lower-case, figures, points and signs, 17 "doubles" (the diphthongs, the "w" and the ampersand, as well as "s" and "f" ligatures), 18 accented sorts (with the acute "é" naturally heavily in the lead) and four superior letters ("a", "e", "o", "r").

Finally, Chapter XVII ("Typographical Points") presented, with a detailed Table, the perfected form of Fournier's point system, the earlier version of which was described in chapter 2 above. The essence of the system now was its basing on a single unit, the point, in place of the cumbersome lines-and-points (the line being a *nompareille*, or 6pts) of the initial scheme of 1737, as reproduced in the *Modèles* in 1742. Thus Fournier had achieved, as he said, "the gradation of type-bodies by definite and constant units". The two-inch scale at the head of his original table was now described as a scale of 144 pts, with its first 36pt section showing 2pt divisions—the precise difference between the main text sizes of 6, 8, 10, 12 and 14pts. The 144pts were still, of course, the old two inches and Fournier admitted the defect of this printed scale, printed as it was on damped paper. After the appearance of the original scale of 1737, he said, "I noticed that the paper in drying had shrunk, making the scale a little less than its proper length. On this occasion I have guarded against this error by adding enough to compensate for the shrinkage of the paper". This was a pretty rough-and-ready correction and, as Updike said, there could easily be a point variation in the scale between different copies of the *Manuel*. Nevertheless, as Walter Tracy noted, Fournier had made "a great innovation"; *le jeune* himself, criticising the confusion which earlier regulations in the trade had only made worse, could rightly be satisfied that he had been induced "to make order of chaos and introduce system where previously it had never prevailed". It was no idle boast that made him speak of a "master-stroke" (*coup de maître*).[1]

While Fournier's point system was to be supplanted by that of the Didots, as chapter 8 describes below, it notably influenced the equally important British-American system. A standard point system was introduced in the United States in 1872 by Marder, Luse of Chicago; the point

[1] Walter Tracy, *Penrose Annual* (1961), pp. 63-4: Updike, I pp. 26-31.

"movement" spread rapidly and in 1886 the United States Typefounders' Association formally went over from the old bodies to a point system. Interestingly enough, though, they did not adopt the Chicago foundry's basis, but that operated since 1882 by the famous Philadelphia foundry of Mackellar, Smiths and Jordan, who had inherited some Fournier matrices. De Vinne himself suggested that the Mackellar pica, taken as the basis for the new point system, may have been derived from a Fournier *cicéro*. The American point, of 0.0138 inch, was not far from the Fournier point of 0.0135 inch; the Didot point was 0.0148 inch.[1]

[1] The Fournier material bought in Paris by Benjamin Franklin, as related above (page 4) was acquired after his death in 1790 by Binny and Ronaldson, the first permanent typefoundry established in America. In 1833 their plant passed to the firm which in 1860 became Mackellar, Smiths and Jordan. The Fournier *cicéro* mould had been used for casting pica-sized type, and when a point system became the subject of discussion in the United States Mackellar's divided their pica into twelve points.

Fournier's final point system: the first page of the type-scale from the Manuel Typographique *(reduced)*

TABLE GÉNÉRALE
DE LA PROPORTION
des différens Corps de Caractères.

ÉCHELLE FIXE
de 144 points Typographiques.

Numb.	Corps.	Points
1	PARISIENNE.	5
2	NOMPAREILLE.	6
3	MIGNONE.	7
4	PETIT-TEXTE.	8
5	GAILLARDE.	9
6	PETIT-ROMAIN. — 2 Parisiennes.	10
7	PHILOSOPHIE. = 1 Parif. 1 Nom-pareille.	11
8	CICÉRO. — 2 Nomp. = 1 Pari-fienne, 1 Mignone.	12
9	SAINT-AUGUSTIN. — 2 Mignones. = 1 Nompareille, 1 Petit-texte.	14

CHAPTER SEVEN

Typography—one and indivisible

The brilliance of Fournier's exposition of punchcutting, typefounding, his point system, his music innovations, his fount schemes, in Vol I of the *Manuel* was matched by the display of his types which formed the main part of Vol II. Here was the matchless typographical repertory of the "creative and fruitful artist, the master-worker of the eighteenth-century renovation of French typographic material".[1] As we have already noted, Vol II was dated 1766 but in fact was not published until 1768; yet France's "literary men" and printers did not have to wait that long to have before them Vol II's specimens of the great array of types available from the foundry at the corner of the Place de l'Estrapade and the Rue des Postes. At the same time as Vol I (1764) there appeared, in a format identical with the *Manuel*, a specimen book of 170 pages, *Les Caractères de l'Imprimerie par Fournier le jeune*. Unusually for Fournier, this was a pure specimen book, with no introductory matter or notes; but the setting, bordering, and even much of the page-numbering, was the same as in Vol II of the *Manuel*.

The 1764 *Caractères*, in short, was a complete preview of the specimens in Vol II, certain "exotics" and Orientals excepted. Fournier's whole completed range (from 5pt to 96pt) was there, including the total of 377 flowers of all bodies. The index was more copious, in one practical aspect, than the index that later appeared in the *Manuel*; for it listed, under each body-size, all the numerous variants (with page-references) instead of giving a single reference only for *cicéro*, *petit-texte* and the rest. The book

[1] Thibaudeau, *La Lettre de l'Imprimerie*, I p. 300.

as a whole clearly indicates that the principal specimen pages for Vol II had been completed by the time Vol I was published; and it may be that it was put out in something of a hurry. Unlike Vol II of the *Manuel*, the first 128 pages of specimens were printed on one side of the paper; only from p. 129 onward were they backed in the normal way.

What Vol II of the *Manuel* particularly showed was the immense work done by Fournier in devising variants for each of the main text sizes. There were no fewer than 82 body types (including italics) in the *Manuel*; the display sizes were much as in the *Modèles* of 1742, the largest sizes of all being still the old Le Bé founts he had then borrowed from his elder brother; clearly his time had been fully occupied on his masterly manipulation of his texts. *Cicéro*, as the most-used text, showed his maximum of seven variants (which, with three italics, meant a total of ten varieties of 12pt at the printer's disposal).

The subtlety of many of these variants (the "minute gradations" as he put it) was remarkable. In order they were: small face (*petit oeil*), leaving "more interval between the lines, which gives them an air of added lightness and grace, but is rather trying to weak eyes" (as he said in his introduction to the specimens); the normal face (*ordinaire*) "holds the mean between beauty and utility" while medium face (*moyen*) "is slightly bigger, which makes the letters more legible"; this last advantage was still more perceptible in large face (*gros oeil*) "but the lines being closer to one another make the page appear too solid"; the large face Dutch style (*gros oeil gout Hollandais*) contrived "to lessen this overloaded appearance" by "making such large-faced letter light in colour and elongated". To these he added a condensed (*serré*) "a face near the *ordinaire*" which "nevertheless gets in more to the line" and a still more condensed letter, the *poétique*, with long ascenders and descenders (to retain proper line-spacing) but with a closeness of set which "makes it possible to set long lines of verse without the necessity of breaking them".[1]

The only body size to have no variant was the minute *Parisienne* (5pt) and its italic with which the specimens opened. Fournier had cut this in 1756 to satisfy a whim of La Pompadour for a tiny psalm-book (issued the following year). But from *nompareille* (6pt) upwards all text sizes had the

---

[1] Carter, pp. 250–1. For the controversy over Fournier's *poétique* and whether he copied it from Louis Luce (or vice versa), see the long note in Carter, pp. 170–1.

65

large-face variant. Otherwise it was evident that Fournier sensibly had an eye to trade demands—even though he had said that "these various gradations . . . are made as much in the interests of beauty as of utility"— and, in a given size, produced only the variants that were likely to sell. Thus small-face started with *mignonne* (7pt) but was not available in the next size up (*petit-texte*), though that offered a medium and a Dutch-style large-face. There was a medium in *petit-romain* (10pt) but not in *philosophie* (11pt), which nevertheless had a small-face italic, not usually available. Fournier never provided italic equivalents for all his roman variants; thus there were, as we have noted, only three italics (*poétique*, which oddly enough lined badly with its roman and looked more like a small-face, *ordinaire* and large-face) to the seven 12pt romans. *Poétique* was restricted to the four sizes—11, 12, 14 and 16pt (*gros-texte*)—demonstrably able to cover all verse formats, from 16mo to small 4to.[1]

After the types came the luxuriant garden of flowers—more than three times the number shown in the *Modèles* a quarter of a century before—a selection of decorated titlings, with rules, brackets, braces and all sorts of signs (astronomical, mathematical, medical and the like). A good display of Greeks and Hebrews, of ancient Blackletter, of *civilité* and *bâtarde* scripts, of Orientals, added a note of erudition. The Flemish, Fraktur, Schwabacher Blackletter, the Arabic, Syriac, Coptic, Armenian, Amharic, Samaritan among other Orientals were supplied by Fournier's friend Breitkopf at Leipzig, while the old French Blackletter and scripts were Le Bé items from his elder brother's foundry, all duly acknowledged (while a concluding note apologised for any errors there might be in the exotic faces "set and made up abroad").[2] His new music was shown, the pretty *petite* in the 16mo page, the *grosse* and the plain-chants on folding-sheets.

Fournier's survey of European typefoundries has been discussed in chapter 5, since the spirit in which he approached this task seemed so much in accord with that chapter's theme—"A Man of the Enlightenment". The same really applies to the 101 alphabets "of every language" which, with his comments upon them, concluded Vol II. It was a typical eighteenth-century exercise, and if some of the alphabets appear apocry-

[1] Carter, p. xxvi: *Manuel*, Vol. II, *passim*.
[2] Carter, p. 256: *Manuel*, II p. 288.

Title page and Parisienne (5pt) specimen—both reduced—from the 1764 "preview" of the Manuel *Vol II*

phal Fournier disarmed criticism by saying that this section was "rather a curiosity than a serious study". He spread his net uncommonly wide, from old English Court Hand to Cyrillic, from Irish Gaelic to Georgian, from "Bulgarian" (which looked remarkably like Glagolitic) to "Hanscret" (Sanskrit). His appended comments were informative and sensible, discussing among other things the development of writing, the discovery of animal and vegetable dyes for colours, even such oddities as old Greek *boustrophedon*.[1]

Vol II of the *Manuel* eventually appeared in August 1768; its author was a dying man. The "long and most cruel malady" of which his widow later spoke finally carried him off on October 8 of that year. He was only 56. It is hardly necessary to speculate on the medical nature of his lingering and fatal disorder; he had quite simply worked himself to death. Some

[1] Carter, pp. 252–5.

67

flavour of his literally killing exertions can easily be remarked in the passage in the *Manuel* where he spoke of his own foundry. "I began it," he wrote, "in 1736 and it is barely finished in the present year, 1766; which is to say that with hard and almost continuous work it has taken me 29 years to bring it to the state in which it now is. I can claim that it is entirely my own handiwork, since I myself have cut the punches, struck and justi-fied the matrices, and constructed a number of the moulds, including all those of a kind which I invented. There is no precedent since the origin of printing for the making of a complete foundry by a single artist."[1]

But beyond all doubt Fournier had, as Beatrice Warde said, "lived long enough to see his establishment the foremost and the richest of privately-owned foundries in Europe, and . . . he had made more changes in typo-graphy and set a more distinctive personal mark on the printed book than anyone else of his day". The modesty and humanity of the man matched the exemplary skill of the artist-craftsman, as the obituary tributes all testified. The *éloge* of 1770 has been much quoted in this book; but in the year of his death *l'Année Littéraire* commented that "the virtues of the man equalled the merits of the artist" in respect of his "integrity, honesty, candour, simplicity, modesty, humanity, beneficence, charm and confi-dence in social relationships", while he "linked the learning of a consum-mate scientist in his own sphere with the talent of a clever typographer". Many years later Momoro spoke of him as "an artist in whom pride in his success never corrupted his heart. He made giant strides on the road of fortune" but "never forgot, even at his most prosperous, that he owed his wealth to his own labours".[2]

Fournier's single-mindedness—and, indeed, single-handedness—made his work, as Thibaudeau said, "the rarest example of typographic unity". "The feeling one gets is that *everything hangs together*: signs, flowers, French and foreign types . . . one feels that the same hand designed and cut the lot." Harry Carter was inspired by the same thought, but expressed it in greater detail, making indeed the most perceptive and most permanent epitaph to Fournier *le jeune* that exists. He wrote: "The real glory of

---

[1] Updike, I pp. 254–6: Carter, p. 266. Of Fournier's chronic overwork a contempor-ary said that his "obstinate application was really the source of his illness, and finally rendered the advice or help of physicians useless" (quoted Updike, I p. 255).

[2] Warde, p. 42: Momoro, *op. cit.*, pp. 215–16, 104.

Fournier's work is the congruity of all its parts. Starting with a conception of the book as a whole, he disciplined every element—roman, italic and script types, decorated titlings, music and ornaments to conform with it. The stylistic unity of his output justifies the emphasis laid in his writings on the ideal of Typography—one and indivisible. His loyalty to it makes him one of the great book-architects with Aldus, Estienne, Elzevir, Baskerville, F. A. Didot and William Morris. He was unique in that he not only designed the materials for his ideal book but made them himself, uniting in his own person the typographic trinity—punchcutter, founder, and printer".[1]

[1] Thibaudeau, I p. 295: Carter, pp. xx–xxi.

Fournier-style flowers from Bodoni's Fregi e Majuscole *(1771) discussed on p. 71*

69

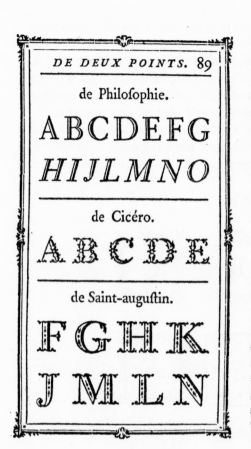

Fournier (1768), left, and Bodoni (1771) fancy capitals

Bodoni poster types from the Manuale Tipografico *(1818): cf. Fournier's* grosses de fonte,
p. 14 above

CHAPTER EIGHT

Forever Fournier

In the year of Fournier's death a young Piedmontese type-cutter, the son of a printer, was appointed by Duke Ferdinand of Parma to the not inconsiderable post of Director of the official printing-house of that Royal Duchy. His name was Giambattista Bodoni and his age 28—just half that of the deceased French master. As a lad, young Bodoni had made his way from his North Italian village to Rome, where he was apprenticed in the press of the Propaganda Fide (the "happy school" he called it). His happy days there, which included early training in punch-cutting, came to an end with the tragic suicide of his benefactor, Ruggeri, the Director of the establishment. Unable to find work in Rome, Bodoni was on his way to seek employment in England—the fame of Baskerville in particular was already echoing round Europe—when he got the Parma offer.

Bodoni was an enthusiastic Fournierist and his first task at the *Stamperia Reale* was to import a substantial stock of Fournier types and ornaments from Paris. Three years later he issued his first specimen (1771), the *Fregi e Majuscole incise e fuse da Giambattista Bodoni*—"Ornaments and Capitals cut and cast by G. B. Bodoni". The types, especially the decorated capitals, the ornaments, borders, indeed the entire presentation was in the manner of Fournier, closely imitating the pages of the *Manuel*. As Updike rather primly noted, the 1771 specimens exhibit Bodoni's "admiration for Fournier, whom he copied in a flattering but barefaced manner". But Bodoni himself made no concealment of the fact that he was basing his work on Fournier; he gloried in it. In the "Typographic Essay" with which he introduced the specimens he said that "the types in which this essay is printed are a derivation of those of Fournier".[1]

Bodoni's subsequent development of his characteristic "modern" style, in line with that of the Didots, need not concern us here; even in these later and very different stages, though, there were still signs of Fournier's influence, as in Bodoni's italic script of 1787 (which greatly pleased Benjamin Franklin) or even some of the extra-large capitals in the posthumous *Manuale Tipografico* of 1818, which have a distinct flavour of Fournier's 1742 *grosses de fonte*. Yet these were no more than lingering whiffs of Fournier; by the time Bodoni had made the Ducal printing-house one of the show-places of Europe, visited by all the nobility and gentry in the course of the Grand Tour, Fournier had ceased to be a name to conjure with; when Arthur Young, agricultural pioneer and indefatigable traveller, called in December 1789, his comment on the "many works of singular beauty" in Signore Bodoni's "celebrated" printing-house was that "the types, I think, exceed those of Didot at Paris". Similarly with a late eighteenth-century Venetian specimen book, that of the Zatta family (1794); while their introductory observations showed that they had studied Fournier's *Manuel* and a number of their borders were Fournier-derived, they made no mention of him. The founder-printers they listed included Bodoni himself, Baskerville and (for France) the Didots.[2]

By the end of the eighteenth century Fournier had been overshadowed by the great Didot dynasty. As typefounders, printers, innovators in papermaking, publishers, the linked Didot families set their mark in a quite unprecedented fashion on French typography. The first "modern" face, produced by François Ambroise Didot in 1784, may be taken as the great turning-point to this new style—the end of the "transitionals" so brilliantly represented by Fournier and Baskerville. Fournier's point system was supplanted by F. A. Didot's system; or perhaps "improved" would be the better word. Didot retained Fournier's duodecimal proportion, with 72 points to the inch, but he substituted a fixed legal standard for the inch—

[1] Updike, I pp. 184ff: Morison describes how Bodoni, taking over the Parma post, "introduced type and ornaments new to Italy. They came from Fournier, who ranks with Bodoni as a principal formative influence of the century; and before all as a typographical pioneer" (*A Tally of Types*, p. 61).

[2] Updike, I pp. 167–8, figs. 307a, 311: II p. 164, I p. 186.

the twelfth part of the official foot, or *pied du roi*—for Fournier's uncertain printed two-inch, 144pt, scale. There was considerable resistance, especially in the French provinces, to the Didot system, and the Fournier point was adhered to until well on in the nineteenth century; it long lingered, as the *mediaan* system, in parts of Belgium.[1]

The eclipse of Fournier was not only the result of the domination of the Didots and their development of a typographic style so much to the taste of the Revolutionary and Napoleonic era; it was evidently encouraged by the total disappearance, or dispersal, of his foundry and all its material, which we have already mentioned. The survival of one size of his *gros-texte* (16pt) roman and italic at the Plantin-Moretus Museum at Antwerp and one size of his *Bâtarde Coulée* at the Reichsdruckerei in Berlin, recorded by Harry Carter, is no more than a happy historical accident. When Pierre Capelle published his *Manuel de la Typographie Française* in 1826 (an elegant quarto—set in a Didot face, of course) he gave Fournier his due place, praising specially his italics and observing that in all his work he was "ever the artist"; but Capelle had great difficulty in finding any Fournier type in Paris to set an appropriate specimen, and he apologised because the only fount he came across was distinctly worn.[2]

The monolithic "modern" typography of the nineteenth century was eventually challenged in France, as it had somewhat earlier been in England (with the Pickering-Whittingham revival of Caslon Old Face in the 1840s). In 1855 Louis Perrin of Lyons brought out some inscriptional capitals and an old-face book fount which was seen to most agreeable effect in the Jouaust series of French classics. Though Perrin's italic has been interestingly described as "derived from Grandjean and Fournier"[3] it could in no way be regarded as a Fournier revival; and Perrin's imitators, headed by the typefounder Theophile Baudoire, produced a supposedly old face letter which they oddly and inaccurately called Elzevir (for many years there was a Linotype version called Old Style No 33) so that *caractères elzéviriennes* became the French trade name for any debased letter of old-face provenance. All this would have infuriated Fournier; while by the turn of the century other deviations from

[1] Updike, I pp. 31–32.
[2] Carter, pp. 271n, 273n: Capelle, p. 68n.
[3] Morison, *On Type Designs* (1962 ed), p. 64.

73

Didot were either the revival of the old classics—the supposed Garamond (Jannon) and Grandjean—or *art nouveau*-inspired oddities like Auriol, Robur or Grasset.

Yet throughout there were never lacking those who kept green the memory of the man who wrote the *Manuel Typographique*. In the France of the 1790s Momoro's textbook, so pompously pooh-poohed by Updike, could still gratefully lean on the *Manuel Typographique* and the erudition of its author. In the 334 text pages of Momoro's work there are no fewer than 71 references to Fournier, mainly to the *Manuel*. Momoro cited Fournier on matters such as fount schemes, music-type, on mathematical, medical, astronomical and other signs (which he simply reproduced from the *Manuel*). A note on an earlier page has quoted Momoro's special praise of Fournier's italics; and he remarked how much he was honoured to be the great man's relative (it will be recalled, from chapter 1, that he had married Fournier's great-niece). It is significant, in those days of growing Didot domination, that Momoro still referred readers, wishful to understand the beauties of the various types, to the *Manuel Typographique*—"a most estimable work, as much for the extent of its knowledge, its principles, its instructions and the masterpieces that it contains, as for the fact that M. Fournier was a truly talented man".[1]

In America a copy of the *Manuel* was in the possession of the expatriate Scots partners Archibald Binny and James Ronaldson, who started their typefoundry in Philadelphia in 1796; the business later became the well-known nineteenth century foundry Mackellar, Smiths and Jordan, taken over by the present American Typefounders Company in 1892. In Britain the Rev Dr Thomas Dibdin, noted bibliophile of the romantic or antiquarian sort, and a founder-member of the Roxburghe Club (he was a nephew of Charles Dibdin, song-writer, playwright and associate of Garrick), wrote in 1809 in his *Bibliomania*: "Fournier's Typographical Manual should be in every printing office". His remark was quoted by Bigmore and Wyman in the first volume (1884) of their great *Bibliography of Printing*, which has an extensive, though far from exhaustive, listing of Fournier. Talbot Baines Reed, the scholar-typefounder—and noted writer of adventure stories for boys—whose *History of the Old English Letter-Foundries* appeared in 1887, said that the descriptions in the *Manuel* of

[1] Momoro, *Manuel de l'Imprimeur* (1796), pp. 103-4.

punchcutting and typefounding "might still serve as an up to date manual of this branch of the art".[1] And when Legros and Grant published their famous *Typographical Printing Surfaces* in 1916 it had a double dedication, to Joseph Moxon and Pierre Simon Fournier *le jeune*—as the only two men who had attempted "with the best contemporary knowledge available, to grapple with the problems of the subject".

The real rediscovery of Fournier's types, the realisation that he was vastly more than a creator of flowers and *lettres de fantaisie*, can be ascribed to the detailed, if sometimes unenthusiastic, treatment of *le jeune* in Updike's monumental *Printing Types*, first published in 1922. This celebrated work was based on the author's lectures at Harvard from 1911-1916, but it is evident that whatever he then said about Fournier found no response from American type specialists, briskly engaged in the first big revival of classic faces. Immediately before and during the First War the Americans produced Bodoni versions, Cloister (based on Jenson), Baskerville and were working on Garamond (Jannon); but there was no sign of Fournier.

James Moran says that "since reading Updike, Stanley Morison had long wanted to revive one of Pierre Simon Fournier's type-faces" and eventually secured a decision by the Monotype Corporation, of which he had been typographical adviser since 1923, to proceed with the recutting for machine composition of a Fournier roman and italic; the model taken was the *St Augustin* (14pt) *ordinaire* shown in the *Manuel Typographique*. Oddly enough there appear still to have been considerable confusions in Morison's mind about Fournier; in 1923 he wrote that *le jeune* "purchased in 1736 the Le Bé foundry" (as we know, this was done by his elder brother, and the date was 1730) and limited himself to showing some of Fournier's shaded and decorated letters—unaccountably dated 1746— which he described as "of very various merit".[2]

In 1924, Morison later recalled, the work on Fournier started—it was thus one of the early Monotype revivals, following the Garamond and the Baskerville—and was completed in 1925. For some reason that is now quite unclear (many Monotype records were destroyed during the late war)

[1] Quoted in *A Tally of Types*, p. 14.

[2] Moran, *Stanley Morison: his typographic achievement* (London: Lund Humphries, 1971) p. 104: Morison and Holbrook Jackson, *A Brief Survey of Printing History* (1923) pp. 50, 62.

two different cuttings were made. One was the Fournier series 185 which has for so long been "Fournier" to the trade; the other, stronger in colour and in its general robustness thought by experts to be the superior version, was numbered 178 and given the name of Barbou to distinguish it. Why was the better reproduction passed over in favour of 185—a light, open face, fairly modest on its body—which Harry Carter sorrowfully said "preserves little of the character of the original"?[1]

The whole affair is mystifying. More than 30 years later Morison referred to the incident with the words "owing to some confusion (due to the typographical adviser's absence abroad) series 185 was approved". This hardly seems an adequate explanation of the failure to secure a sound decision when such care had been taken to cut two different versions. The typographical adviser could easily have been consulted, by post or telephone, had there been the desire to do so. Here, indeed, the answer may lie. The Monotype Corporation was not without its internal politics; and in all technical matters, such as punchcutting and matrix-stamping for new founts, the Monotype works manager, Frank H. Pierpont, was the autocrat whose word was law. Pierpont was a technician, first and last, surrounded by like-minded technicians; he could not stand outside non-technical advisers and was known to think Morison's ideas "a lot of rot". It seems most likely, therefore, that with Morison out of the way, Pierpont arbitrarily plumped for series 185.[2]

What must seem curious to a later generation is that this peculiar situation was so calmly accepted. For many years the incident remained virtually unknown to the wider world of print. The one size of Barbou was used by the Cambridge University Press for the last three numbers of *The Fleuron*; not till 1959 was the 12pt cut, for an American edition of Benjamin Franklin's papers; only in 1967 was the full composition range, from 8pt upwards, made available. Whether, as time goes on, the superior 178 will supplant 185 remains to be seen; the notion may be hazarded that the somewhat esoteric name Barbou—however apt a tribute to the man who used Fournier's types so well—is a little offputting. Other Monotype

[1] Moran, ibid: Carter, p. xxxiii: Barbou 178 has a greater x-height than Fournier 185, most noticeable in the 8 and 9pt sizes, while certain letters are differently drawn—the cap M is slightly splayed and the lower-case w has crossed arms.

[2] Moran, p. 93.

series with a number of variants (Bodoni, for instance) are simply distinguished by the different number following the generic designation. The
same might surely have been done with Fournier, possibly calling it in
addition Fournier No. 2.

Despite Harry Carter's criticism (and in the same passage he admitted
it to be a "useful type") Fournier 185 became popular with many publishers
and book printers. Its element of condensation, plus its elegance (notably
in its italics), met a real need. The Monotype Corporation sold more than
160 sets of 12pt matrices, with 11pt and 10pt next in order of demand.
Presenting specimens of the first range of sizes (10, 12, $13\frac{1}{2}$, 14 and 18pt,
roman with italic), the March–June 1926 double number of the *Monotype
Recorder* contained a "Notice to the Reader" from the Corporation com-
mending this "first use of that much-needed face—a new condensed letter.
Though condensed it is well-proportioned, and in spite of the obvious
modernity of its design, it keeps the elegance of the old faces".

That number of the *Recorder* was filled with a magnificent monograph
by Beatrice Warde (Paul Beaujon) on Fournier and eighteenth-century
French typography. It followed up, and improved on, Updike and it has
been frequently cited in this book. Four years later Harry Carter produced
Fournier on Typefounding, a translation of the *Manuel*, with an introduction
and notes (and including not only the *Manuel*'s plates but the *Avis* to the
Modèles of 1742); this remains in many ways the peak of modern Fournier
scholarship and has been indispensable for the present work. As it was
published in 1930 in a limited edition of 200 copies only it has inevitably
become a collector's item of great rarity. More recently the Introductory
Supplement by James Mosley to the 1965 facsimile of the *Modèles* has
thrown new light on Fournier's early work; it may be noted that this
facsimile was the work of a London firm, the Eugrammia Press, which
should put the French to shame. It is extraordinary that a unique work like
the *Manuel Typographique* was never republished in its native land; nor
has it so far been produced in facsimile.

As already said, Fournier 185 came to be widely used. Display sizes
up to 48pt were cut, and the Oxford University Press, among others, made
good use of these sizes on book jackets as well as for large drop initials.
Fournier for text was elegantly exploited by Chatto and Windus, it was
adopted by R. & R. Clark of Edinburgh for the standard collected edition

of Bernard Shaw (Constable), and in recent years it has made an attractive show in the Penguin Books anthologies of foreign poetry. It made a great hit in Czechoslovakia (the diacritical signs necessary for Czech were exceptionally well cut by Monotype) and has been extensively used by leading Prague printers for the high-quality bookwork in which they have long excelled. It can be seen, for instance, in the major typographical study by Oldrich Hlavsa and Frantisek Sedlacek, *Tipograficka Pisma Latinkova* (Prague 1957)—"Roman Printing Types"—or its Prague-printed, London-published English version *A Book of Type and Design* (Peter Neville 1961).

The most imposing achievement of Fournier 185, however, was undoubtedly its use by Sir Francis Meynell for the grand seven-volume *Nonesuch Shakespeare*, generally regarded as the masterpiece of the Nonesuch Press. Edited by Herbert Farjeon to the highest textual standards, and with marginal notes, its splendid form amply justified Sir Francis's decision "to use the Fournier type for its combination of elegance and legibility, even in its very small sizes". Sir Francis had to make one change, though, since he found that Fournier's capitals—redesigned, as we have seen, to line with the tops of the ascenders—"delivered a series of optical bangs" in the conditions of Shakespeare's constant capitalisation. Thus, *pace* Pierre Simon, a set of shortened caps (according with the old-face practice he had condemned) was designed to accompany the 185 lower-case for this particular work.[1]

Somehow it is pleasant to reflect that a master of the French eighteenth century, many of whose contemporaries thought Shakespeare "barbarous", should have been the source of so apt a typographic form for a Shakespeare edition the like of which may never be seen again. It goes to show, as Beatrice Warde said, that what we find in Fournier types is "the agelessness of reasonable design and the charm of a learned artisan who loved to hold the tool".[2] If a musical analogy were sought, might we not add that Fournier *le jeune* could well rank as the Mozart of typography?

[1] Francis Meynell, *My Lives* (London: The Bodley Head, 1971) p. 172.
[2] Warde, p. 43.

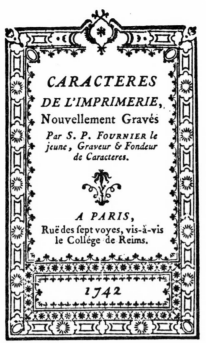

CARACTERES DE L'IMPRIMERIE, Nouvellement Gravés *Par S. P. FOURNIER le jeune, Graveur & Fondeur de Caracteres.*

A PARIS, Ruë des sept voyes, vis-à-vis le Collége de Reims.

1742

AVIS.

CEs Caracteres font gravés dans un goût fuivi & uniforme d'après ce que nous avons de plus beau dans ce genre , en obfervant néanmoins de faire quelques changemens & corrections qui ont paru néceffaires pour leur donner plus de perfection. Ces modéles de Caracteres pourront fervir à Meff. les Imprimeurs & Libraires, pour faire un choix de ceux dont ils auront befoin ; & à ceux d'entre les Auteurs ou Lecteurs curieux qui voudront favoir en lifant un Livre , le nom & la qualité du Caractère avec lequel il eft imprimé. Ils pourront fe procurer ce plaifir , en cherchant dans ce Recueil le Caractere qui aura du rapport en groffeur à celui qu'ils veulent connoître. Le nom eft marqué à chaque, & par ce moyen on pourra facilement acquérir une connoiffance qui jufqu'à préfent eft affez peu commune.

On trouvera dans le Recueil in-quarto , où ces mêmes Caracteres font imprimés plus en grand, diférentes choses qui n'ont pu entrer dans celui-ci , & qui font faites pour l'ornement & la propreté des impressions, comme une nouvelle Collection de Lettres de deux points Romaines & Italiques, des vignettes d'un goût nouveau , des Réglets de fonte de toutes fortes , dont ceux qui enquadrent ces pages peuvent fervir de modéles. On trouvera auffi au commencement du même Recueil un Avis aux amateurs de l'Art de l'Imprimerie avec l'Approbation & la Permission pour l'impression de ces Epreuves.

The reproduction of the 24mo *Caractères* (1742) which follows is actual size and complete, from the St Bride Institute Printing Library copy. It will be recalled that *gros oeil* is "large face". Type-size equivalents are approximately *double canon* 56 point (sometimes taken as 48 point), *gros canon* 44 point (i.e. fractionally above our 42 point), *Trismégiste* 36 point, *petit canon* 28 point, *Palestine* 24 point, *gros parangon* 22 point, *petit parangon* 20 point, *gros romain* 18 point, *gros texte* 16 point, *St Augustin* 14 point, *cicéro* 12 point, *philosophie* 11 point, *petit romain* 10 point, *gaillarde* 9 point, *petit texte* 8 point, *mignone* 7 point, *nompareille* 6 point.

Dieu soit aimé & Adoré

Qu'il le soit éternel- lement.

Peu de choses amuse la Jeu- neffe.

Rien de durable dans ce monde.

Heureux celui qui ne s'y at- tache pas

En peu de tems nous paffons de la vie à la mort.

L'honneur acquis est caution de celui qu'on acquérera.

Quelque bien que l'on nous dife de nous, on ne nous apprend rien de nouveau

La Sagesse & la réputation ne font pas moins à la mercy de la Fortune que le bien.

La vanité, la honte & furtout le tempérament, font en plufieurs la valeur des hommes & la vertu des fe.

L'orgueil contrepese toutes nos miseres. Car ou il les cache, ou s'il les montre, il fe glorifie de les connoitre.

On ne fauroit conferver les fentimens que l'on doit avoir pour fes amis fi on fe donne la liberté de parler fouvent de leurs défaut

Gros Parangon.

Le defir de mé-
riter les louanges
qu'on nous donne
fortifie notre ver
tu : & celles que
l'on donne à la
valeur, & à l'es-
prit, contribuent
à les augmenter.

Petit Parangon Gros-œil.

Si nous n'avions
point de défauts
nous ne pren-
drions pas tant
de plaifir a en
remarquer dans
les autres.

On parle peu fi
la vanité ne fait
point parler.

Petit Parangon Gros-œil.

Tout le monde fe
plaint de fa mé-
moire , mais per-
sonne ne fe plaint
de fon esprit.

Rien ne fait plus
fentir la misere
des hommes que
l'agitation conti
nuelle de la vie.

Petit Parangon Ordinaire.

L'homme aiant
befoin de la fo-
ciété pour vivre
commodément &
agréablement , il
doit contribuer
au bien de cette
fociété en fe ren-
dant utile à ceux
qui la compofent

Petit Parangon Ordinaire.

Il y a dans le cœur
& dans l'esprit hu-
main une généra-
tion perpétuelle de
passions en forte
que la ruine de
l'une eft presque
toûjours l'établis-
sement d'une autre

Gros Romain.

Tous les fentimens
ont chacun un ton
de voix, des geftes
& des mines qui
leur font propres :
Ce rapport bon ou
mauvais, agréable
ou defagréable, eft
ce qui fait que les
perfonnes plaifent
ou déplaifent.

Gros Romain.

Presque tout le monde prend plaisir à s'aquitter des petites obligations, beaucoup de gens ont de la reconnoissance pour les médiocres, mais il n'y a quasi personne qui n'ait de l'ingratitude pour les grandes.

Gros Texte.

L'homme croit souvent se conduire lors qu'il est conduit ; & pendant que par son esprit il tend à un but son cœur l'entraîne insensiblement à un autre.

Assez de gens méprisent le bien ; mais peu savent le donner comme il faut.

Gros Texte.

Il y a des crimes qui deviennent innocens & même glorieux par leur éclat, leur nombre & leur excès. Il arive de là que les voleries publiques sont des habiletez ; & que prendre des provinces injustement s'appelle faire des conquétes, & des grandes actions.

Saint Augustin.

L'amour de la gloire, la crainte de la honte, le dessein de faire fortune, le desir de rendre notre vie commode & agréable, & l'envie d'abaisser les autres, sont souvent les causes de cette valeur si célébre parmi les hommes.

C'est la prospérité qui donne des amis, mais c'est l'adversité qui les éprouve.

Saint Augustin.

Il y a beaucoup de gens qui ressemblent aux vaudevilles que tout le monde chante un certain temps, quelque fades & dégoûtans qu'ils soient.

Si la vanité ne renverse pas entiérement les vertus, du moins elle les ébranle toutes.

Il n'y a guéres d'homme assez habile pour connoître tout le mal qu'il fait.

CICERO GROS ŒIL.

Les humeurs du corps ont un cours ordinaire & réglé qui meut & tourne imperceptiblement notre volonté ; elles roulent ensemble & exercent successivement un empire secret en nous : de sorte qu'elles ont une part considérable à toutes nos actions sans que nous le puissions connoître.

L'orgueil ne veut pas devoir, & l'amour propre ne veut pas payer.

CICERO MOYEN.

LA félicité eft dans le goût & non pas dans les chofes: & c'eft par avoir ce qu'on aime qu'on eft heureux, & non par avoir ce que les autres trouvent aimable.

Il eft de la reconnoiffance comme de la bonne foy des marchans : elle entretient le commerce: & nous ne payons pas parce qu'il eft plus jufte de nous acquiter, mais pour trouver plus facilement des gens qui nous prêtent.

CICERO.
Dernier gravé.

Qu'on choififfe telle condition qu'on voudra, & qu'on y affemble les biens & les fatisfactions qui femblent pouvoir contenter un homme. Si celui qu'on aura mis dans cet état eft fans occupation, & qu'on le laiffe faire réflexion fur ce qu'il eft, cette félicité languiffante ne le foutiendra pas, il tombera dans des vuës affligeantes de l'avenir, & fi on ne l'occupe hors de lui, le voilà néceffairement malheureux.

CICERO ITALIQUE.

IL faut gouverner la fortune comme la fanté, en jouir quand elle eft bonne, prendre patience qand elle eft mauvaife, & ne faire jamais de grands remedes fans un extrême befoin.

C'eft une ennuyeuse maladie que de conferver fa fanté par un trop grand régime.

Il y a des gens qu'on aprouve dans le monde, qui n'ont pour tout mérite que les vices qui fervent au commerce de la vie.

PHILOSOPHIE.

L'orfque les grands hommes fe laiffent abattre par la longueur de leurs infortunes ils font voir qu'ils ne les foûtenoient que par la force de leur ambition, & non par celle de leur ame, & qu'à une grande vanité près, les Héros font faits comme les autres hommes.

Nous fommes fi préoccupés en notre faveur, que fouvent ce que nous prenons pour des vertus ne font que des vices qui leur reffemblent, & que l'amour propre nous déguife.

PETIT ROMAIN GROS ŒIL.

IL eft du véritable amour comme de l'apparition des efprits : tout le monde en parle, mais peu de gens en ont vu.

ON ne peut fe confoler d'être trompé par fes ennemis, & trahi par fes amis ; & l'on eft fouvent fatisfait de l'être par foi-même.

ON ne méprife pas tous ceux qui ont des vices ; mais on méprife tous ceux qui n'ont aucune vertu.

PETIT ROMAIN ORDINAIRE.

Nous fommes fi préfomptueux, que nous voudrions être connus de toute la terre. Et nous fommes fi vains, que l'eftime de cinq ou fix perfonnes qui nous environnent, nous amufe & nous contente.

Malgré la vue de toutes les miferes qui nous tiennent à la gorge, nous avons un inftinct que nous ne pouvons réprimer, qui nous éleve.

La douceur de la gloire eft fi grande, qu'à quelque chofe qu'on l'attache, même à la mort on l'aime.

PETIT ROMAIN ITALIQUE.

Les grands & les petits ont mêmes accidens, mêmes fâcheries, & mêmes passions. Mais les uns sont au haut de la roue & les autres près du centre, & ainsi moins agités par les mêmes mouvemens.

Jamais on ne fait le mal si pleinement & si gayement, que quand on le fait par un faux principe de conscience.

Ce qui nous rend la vanité des autres insupportable, c'est qu'elle blesse la nôtre.

L'hypocrisie est un hommage que le vice rend à la vertu.

GAILLARDE.

L'amour est une passion de l'appetit concupiscible qui se porte au bien sensible, conçû tel par l'imagination, & l'amitié est une vertu qui porte notre volonté au bien honnête, conçû tel par l'entendement. Le premier est souvent contraire a l'autre, car les passions violentes trouble la raison, & l'excès d'amour dégénere en jalousie ; au lieu que l'amitié ne peut avoir d'excès & qu'elle mérite d'autant mieux le nom d'amitié, qu'elle est extrême.

Ne voyez point de femmes, conseil bouru ; voyez les femmes, & n'aimez jamais, conseil inutile ; voir les femmes & prendre des précautions contre l'amour, c'est vivre en homme sage, & en homme poli.

PETIT TEXTE GROS-ŒIL.

Tous les hommes vivent comme s'ils avoient fait entr'eux une convention de se tromper, de se nuire, de se déchirer ; la convention est tacite, mais elle est générale. On avouë bien qu'il seroit plus beau dans l'ordre des choses de voir une même bonté, une même sincérité, une même probité, faire cette uniformité de conduite ; mais parce que le grand nombre est gâté, on ne veut pas se corriger seul, de crainte d'être la duppe des autres.

PETIT TEXTE ORDINAIRE.

LES honneurs, l'autorité & les richesses ne méritent pas d'être comptées parmi les biens, parce qu'elles n'ont d'autre utilité que celle que les hommes y attachent. Que me sert en effet la possession de plusieurs terres, si une seule de grandeur médiocre suffit à mon nécessaire, & me donne un air aussi libre à respirer ? l'autorité sur les autres hommes apporteroit-elle plus de calme à mon esprit ? toutes les perles de l'Orient jointes à tout l'or des Indes, ne rendroient pas mon sommeil plus doux ni ma santé plus robuste.

C'est le jugement sain, le bon esprit, le bon cœur, en un mot, c'est la sagesse, & non pas le bien, qui nous procure par la tranquillité de l'ame la véritable abondance, le vrai bonheur & les vrais plaisirs.

PETIT TEXTE ITALIQUE.

La pluspart des maniéres que l'art a introduites en Europe, ont quelque chose de fatiguant pour des esprits naturels : ces révérences de theatres, ces gestes outrés qui expriment des transports lorsqu'il ne s'agit que des sentimens : ces louanges prodiguées, ces fausses protestations de services, ces affectations de visage riant où la joye paroît contrainte, ces airs contrefaits de bonté & de cordialité, où l'on entrevoit quelque chose de géné & de farouche; vains artifices des hommes, qui font les charmes du vulgaire & le mépris des gens de bien.

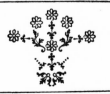

MIGNONE.

Dans un lieu du bruit retiré,
Où pour peu qu'on soit modéré,
On peut trouver que tout abonde,
Sans amour sans ambition,
Exempt de toute passion,
Je jouis d'une paix profonde ;
Et pour m'assûrer le seul bien
Que l'on doit estimer au monde,
Tout ce que je n'ai pas, je le compte
pour rien.

Le tems d'un insensible cours,
Nous porte à la fin de nos jours ;
C'est à notre sage conduite,
Sans murmurer de ce défaut,
De nous consoler de sa fuite,
En le ménageant comme il faut.

NOMPAREILLE.

La fanté de l'ame n'eft pas plus affû-
rée que celle du corps ; & quoique
l'on paroiffe éloigné des paffions, on
n'eft pas moins en danger de s'y laif-
fer emporter , que de tomber malade
quand on fe porte bien.

Les défauts de l'ame font comme les
bleffures du corps ; quelque foin que
l'on prenne , la cicatriceparoît toûjours, & elles font à tout moment en
danger de fe r'ouvrir.

*Détromper un homme préoccupé de fon
mérite c'eft lui rendre un auffi mauvais
fervice que celui que l'on rendit à ce fou
d'Athenes qui croyoit que tous les vaif-
feaux qui arrivoient dans le port, étoient
à lui.*
*L'homme aime la malignité & la fatire ;
ce n'eft pas contre les malheureux , mais
contre les heureux fuperbes ; & c'eft fe
tromper que d'en juger autrement.*

HEBREUX.

הללו את יהוה, כל
גוים שכחוהו כל
דאמים : כי גבר
עלינו חסדו ואמת
יהות לעולם הללו יה

הללו את יהוה כל גוים
שכחוהו כל דאמים • כי גבר
עלינו חסדו ואמת יהות לעולם
הללו יה :

On trouvera
dans la même
Fonderie ,
les autres
caracteres de
l'Imprimerie.